EILEEN

Also by Eileen O'Casey
SEAN

EILEEN

EILEEN O'CASEY

EDITED WITH AN INTRODUCTION BY
J. C. TREWIN

ST. MARTIN'S PRESS
175 Fifth Avenue
New York, N.Y. 10010

M

SBN 333 13472 9

First published 1976 by
MACMILLAN LONDON LIMITED
4 Little Essex Street London WC2R 3LF
and Basingstoke
Associated companies in New York Dublin
Melbourne Johannesburg and Delhi

Printed in Great Britain by
THE BOWERING PRESS LTD
Plymouth

PR
6029
C3
Z52
1976

To my Grandchildren
Oona, Duibhne, and Brendan O'Casey
and Ruben Kenig

Contents

Contents

List of Illustrations

Acknowledgements

I WOULD like to express my thanks to Lady Hardman Earle (Maie Drage), Mrs Alison Gaunt, Mrs Laurence Kenig (Shivaun O'Casey), Miss Ella Winter; Mr Brooks Atkinson, Mr William Elmhirst (Dartington Hall), Mr Harold Macmillan, Mr Breon O'Casey, Mr J. J. O'Leary, Mr John O'Riordan, Captain H. P. Sears, R.N. (retd), the authorities of Trinity College, Dublin; and, for their secretarial help, Mrs Sheila O'Higgins, and Miss Ros Moore.

E. O'C.

Introduction

EILEEN O'CASEY was born in the city of Dublin and to Dublin she has returned. She lives today in what, seen from the garden gate, looks illusively like a house only a single storey high. But, once the front door is opened, you find that the house spreads on, developing unexpectedly as you get into it. That is, in a sense, like Eileen O'Casey's own life as it moved out from the fettering restrictions of her youth: the tale of a beautiful young actress, convent-bred and delighting in the sophistication of the West End of London during the 1920s, who married one of Ireland's greatest dramatists, a man much older than herself, brought up in the tenements of Dublin. Eileen and Sean lived together through the ardours and endurances of nearly forty years. All but ten were spent surprisingly in the deep south-west of England at Totnes and St Marychurch outside Torquay.

As the marriage matured, so Eileen's character grew. Ever responsive and warm-hearted, she did miss, at first sorely, the freedom she had had as an actress (sometimes, too, as a model) which repaid her for a childhood of frustration. Though for a time she continued her career on the stage, it could not last. Half regretful, but a basically devoted wife and mother, she turned inward to her family. She had to keep together a household in which money was usually short; to aid a husband momentarily cast down by the theatre's sharp neglect; and to adapt herself to a mid-Devon world the O'Caseys would never have dreamed of if Bernard Shaw had not told them of the progressive school at

Dartington. That would be right for the boys, said G.B.S., a ready adviser, and to Devon the family went.

The storm of the Second World War affected Eileen O'Casey less than it might have done, for at Totnes she would use in various ways her commonsense and her organising power, her gifts of laughter and friendship. Then, the war over, she had to watch her indefatigable husband down the slant of life. In the end near-blindness was approaching, a grief for Sean who lived among his books, and who loved 'colour and stir' (even his titles are revealing, *Purple Dust*, *The Silver Tassie*, *Red Roses For Me*, *The Green Crow*, *Under a Colored Cap*). More and more he depended on Eileen: never was a wife so needed. He was seventy-five when they had to meet the agonising loss of their second son, Niall, who died of leukaemia. Living outside Torquay (in Sean's words 'looking over the tops of many trees . . . to the green cliffs of Babbacombe'), and away, irrevocably, from the London she so wistfully desired, Eileen had to accommodate herself to a quiet to-and-fro, a domestic routine at odds with the eagerness of her nature, her love of life.

True, from time to time, as she says in her book, she had her holidays. One at least was rare: a journey, on behalf of Sean, to New York, where his later work (as it would be in Europe) was honoured more than in England. With Ireland – where *The Bishop's Bonfire* was acted, under Tyrone Guthrie, in 1955 – there had to be the lingering feud that Yeats's rejection of *The Silver Tassie* had strengthened. Sean died in 1964. 'In eighty-four years of unselfish living,' said Brooks Atkinson finely, 'it was the first time his heart had failed him.' By then it was getting on for half his life since Eileen, overcome by her reading of *Juno and the Paycock* in New York ('Take away this murdherin' hate, and give us Thine own eternal love!'), had returned to London determined to meet the dramatist – an Elizabethan re-born in his dialogue and his conduct of the stage.

II

After Sean's death Eileen had at once to create her own new world. She found a London utterly transformed since she had left their Battersea flat in the autumn before the war. She had to discover new friends; to come to terms, if she could – and it was not easy – with the 'inner loneliness' that had long haunted her and become more oppressive. This theme runs through her book. It derives from childhood in a home that was never a home but a procession of furnished rooms; and from the holidays she had to spend either in grey Fulham bed-sitters or at her Essex convent school because her mother was at work. She had wanted companionship then. In later life – always, indeed, since she had been on the stage as Eileen Carey – she felt round eight o'clock in the evening that somewhere a curtain was rising and that she should be there. The evening had been Sean's high time for work; it had been hers and was no longer. But, after his death, and with no one at all in the house, she found that her loneliness was sharper still.

Through her life she had remembered her upbringing and what it did to her. A sensitive and impressionable schoolgirl, she hated condescension but was naturally competitive. Her mother, narrow and exigent, insisted on a daughter's duty. Eileen fulfilled it to the last, though she had missed the sure and loving warmth which should be any child's right and which she gave to her own children.

In her first book (1971) she concentrated upon Sean. Now she speaks more freely about herself as well. She describes in ampler detail such things as the orphanage and convent discipline of the formative years, her tour as a D'Oyly Carte chorus girl when the company after the First World War was at its meridian, and the comradeship of *Bitter Sweet* – which was not a play Sean admired in spite of his respect for its impresario, Cochran. At the close we have something of her life since Sean died: her London homes in Kensington and on the Hampstead hill; the visits to East Germany and Czechoslovakia; the search for renewal; the cause of the final move to Eire.

Sean and *Eileen* stand together as the tale of an astonishing union and its epilogue. A vivacious talker (and you must imagine the amusement in those blue eyes), she relishes her set-pieces as she remembers the correspondence course in the Ursuline convent – 'It is lovely to see the daffodils showing themselves' – the explosive geyser in St John's Wood, the agony of the unpaid restaurant bill with her theatre curtain almost ready to rise, the Parisian adventure with her daughter Shivaun, the complications of a 'cure' at Marienbad.

III

It is Eileen's book, and yet inevitably we must return again and again to Sean, who is recalled, in speech and behaviour, with such exact affection. We ought also to speak of Eileen as Sean knew her. In his last letter, written a month before he died, and begun in hospital,* he said: 'Wherever you are, darling, is home to me. When you leave here for a week to do business in London, the home is shadowed till you come back to me . . . The stalwart of the O'Casey home is not Sean, but Eileen; so it is, so it was always.'

Here she is now, settled – as in his heart I think he might have liked her to be – in an inconspicuously elegant Irish house. Within, Sean's portrait is on the wall. Sean's books are upon the shelves. Not far off is the city Sean wrote of so often, for better, for worse, for richer, for poorer; the city of *Juno* and the *Plough*; the city of four autobiographical books; the city beneath a 'sulky green tent that Dublin called the sky'; the 'gold-speckled candle white as snow' that was 'yellowish now, leanin' sideways, and guttherin' down to a last shaky glimmer in the wind of life,' but also, and ever, the city that could be in 'th' grip o' God,' the city of the invocation in *Red Roses For Me*:

* *Sean*, p. 291.

'Home of th' Ostmen, of th' Norman, and th' Gael, we greet you!'

This was Eileen's birthplace. It was Sean's. Now the years have fallen away.

Hampstead, 1976   J. C. Trewin

CHAPTER ONE

Childhood

WHAT on earth, then, do I remember? First, possibly, from my childhood, the furnished rooms I lived in with my mother: bed-sitters mostly, sometimes a sitting-room and a bedroom. One I think of especially, in West London near Brook Green, Hammersmith: a large room with a large double bed – for usually I shared my mother's – a table in the middle, a sideboard, a dressing-table, a washstand with its jug and basin (they would probably fetch fantastic prices now), and one cosy armchair. Maybe in better days it had been the drawing-room of the house or the best bedroom. The essential gas stove was in either an enclosure on the landing, or a small room down a few steps from the bathroom my mother insisted we must have: certainly in this I would take after her. In bed at night one could be secure in a compact little world with that remote, indefinable after-the-meal feeling. From my bed I could see the cruet on the sideboard and the cupboard beneath where the marmalade and sauces were kept. Meat and butter, the perishables, would be in a wire safe outside a north window. Everything about my mother had to be spotless, for she was almost passionately clean and expected others to be.

She must have been sad about her progress from one shabby house to another, respectable though they were. In her Irish family home at Belmullet, in the north-east corner of County Mayo, she had had servants and comfort and security, and, after her marriage, her own home and coloured servants in South Africa. As a handsome, convent-bred girl, Kathleen Carey, she

had persuaded her family to let her leave for Dublin in order
to train as a nurse. It was in a boarding-house there that she
met Edward Reynolds, my father, who came of farming stock
from Athlone in County Westmeath and had left the farm to
study in Dublin, taking with him his share of the inheritance
as the eldest son. Because my mother's family objected to
Edward – 'not a good match,' they said – he sailed off to South
Africa to make his money; after two years as an accountant
with a mining firm in Johannesburg, he sent for Kathleen, en-
closing the money for her fare and trousseau. They were married and settled down comfortably; and two boys were born.
The elder son died practically after birth; the younger, when
the Boer War began, my mother brought back with them to
Ireland. I was born in Dublin, but we could not stay there because my father, invariably restless, gambled away what means
we had; in the end we had to cross over to London to live in
furnished rooms. My mother became dangerously ill with rheu-
matic fever, and it was during this illness, when she could not
leave her bed, that my little brother died of bronchitis: a fearful shock, for she had loved him dearly and some part of her
died with him – I was forever second-best. My father, certain
that he would get work in South Africa, resolved, now that the
war was over, to go back to his old firm in Johannesburg and to
send enough every month to support us.

Meanwhile we lived in our series of lodgings. Perhaps my
mother kept on searching for a home of her own – I don't
know. Still, I was never alone, and there would be a room in
which to play and eat and sleep; I do remember a doll and pic-
ture-books and the constant need to be 'tidy' and to clear up
after playing, something that as a born tomboy I found re-
pressive and probably resented. A landlady, or a landlady's
children, would never be good enough for us. My mother talked
about keeping ourselves to ourselves. Bernard Shaw said to me
once, years later, that the poor did have the blessing of companionship, with 'nothing to hide'. Possibly; but in the middle
or upper-middle classes at that time you were never sure of

yourself. You asked what it was all about? Why was he or she
not good enough to talk to? Indeed, the only people at ease
seemed to be either the very poor or the aristocratic.

II

My mother's sister, Aunt Alice Cleary, was often with me in
those days. She was a widow and her late husband, I think,
had been a surgeon in Dublin. Somehow she was down on her
luck, so for a while she stayed with us, having presumably
another room in the house. A 'great dresser', as they called it,
she had a flair for clothes and loved making hats. My mother,
too, delighted in hats with flowers or feathers. Until she died
in 1962 (and her precise age was a mystery to me), she would
contrive somehow to get a new hat for Easter or trim up an old
one; and she never understood how I could go about bare-headed
or simply wear a scarf.

When I was five or six years old my father returned from
South Africa very ill after a sharp nervous breakdown. I can
recollect him now hazily, a tall, good-looking man who used to
take me for bus rides. If you had a breakdown in those days you
were regarded immediately as a borderline case; my father was
not certified – extremely intelligent, he had simply too much
on his mind – but he did go to an institution called the Bethlem
Royal Hospital. My mother, after his return, had been continually nagging him. They could never have lived in peace
together: in some ways they must have been mutually de-
structive, even though he had responded to her beauty as a girl.
He had always this romantic streak; she told me that while
studying accountancy in Dublin, one of his jobs at night was
to do the books of the Gaiety Theatre, and he had fallen in love
from a distance with Ellen Terry who was over in Ireland on
tour. Certainly a romantic; rash, as well, to leave the farm to
seek his education in Dublin. A gambler, he was not – I am pretty

sure – an excessive drinker; my mother would have told me if he was.

Sex she hated; again and again she said it was 'disgusting' without explaining to me why. (No one ever told me.) Moreover, it must have shocked her greatly when my father abandoned his religion after they were married. Utterly rigid, she never dreamed of questioning the faith. If you failed in any part of it, you were 'bad', and that was that: no excuses. With this gap between them they could not possibly have got on.

Accepting, as she had to, that my father was in hospital and unable to support her, she knew she must go out to work. She had not qualified as a nurse, for illness had stopped her after the second year, so there was only one thing for it: a post as a 'nurse-companion', familiar enough when incomes were steadier and richer families could employ someone to help with an elderly person's daily routine – dressing and undressing, washing and meals. That was all right, but she had to live in and what would become of me? She tried several schools – at first, naturally, the grander, more expensive ones, the Sacred Heart and another at Twickenham. At length, though fees had been reduced for her, she saw that there was only one way: I would have to enter an orphanage. Some of her relatives were nuns in the Order, and that was why the Sisters of Charity in Orchard Street, not far from Hyde Park, agreed to take me as a special case, and why on visiting days I would be found unnaturally quiet in the orphanage parlour.

III

Probably, as at all emotional moments after the age of five, I responded without tears or fuss. There were a hundred or more children in the orphanage, and about six of us appeared to be a little 'special'; that is, our mothers paid what they could towards our keep. It was a great change from the old life. Several of the nuns were kind, others were not, but one of them, Sister

Frances, really took to me and loved me. That is something the young cannot do without. (I am sure that, whatever may be said for boarding-schools, a child should have what means so much to it, the security of its own home at night.)

In our dormitories, large and small, rows of iron beds were set neatly on a floor of bare boards, well scrubbed. We were never cold; there were blankets enough, and our nightdresses were of thick white flannelette. Beside the beds we had each a small cupboard for our shoes, a piece of soap – cut from a longer piece and either carbolic or grey-mottled – our flannel, towel and toothbrush, all most hygienic. Every morning, in slippers and dressed up to our petticoats, we went to wash in a large room with rows of back-to-back basins; later we hurried back to the dormitory to put on our dresses which were waisted, with a fairly full skirt, and our dark-coloured pinafores (Sunday dresses were different). Clean clothes were given out weekly from a central cupboard, and once a week we had a bath which was never taken naked, but always under a large shift; the smaller girls were both washed and supervised. Our hair was in plaits. Regularly a nun would go through it with a fine two-sided comb dipped into a saucer of vinegar. They could not have taken more care of our health and cleanliness. In winter we had cod-liver oil and those who needed it had Parrish's food, both doled out morning by morning in a room that was set aside to deal with any small thing you might have wrong with you – I know we got a good many whitlows and chilblains on our fingers. If you needed bandaging or attention, or felt at all sick, you went to this room and were transferred, if necessary, to the sick-bay. We might have been young army recruits, we were watched so closely. I doubt now whether some of the public schools could have improved on it.

Very little could penetrate our defences. If anything did it could have come only from a day school that the nuns ran at the back of the orphanage and that children from the district would use as their own. We got to it through a big room with basins where during the day we washed our hands and faces –

we were not allowed to go upstairs – and then on through a large asphalt yard, also our playground. A nun acted as head-mistress, there were lay teachers, and a priest took us for scripture and religious knowledge generally, subjects that fascinated me as a small child. Obviously we had to do without music or dancing, but I enjoyed the organised games, 'Oranges and lemons', 'Poor Jenny's a-weeping', 'Here we come gathering nuts in May', and 'I sent a letter to my love'. Lots of skipping, of course, over a long rope; and such variations as dropping a handkerchief and picking it up while continuing to skip, and 'Salt, mustard, vinegar, pepper', which meant going slow on the salt, quicker on the mustard, and very quick indeed on the pepper. Some of the older girls excelled in what we called French skipping, for which they used a pair of ropes and jumped from one to the other.

Our food was ample, plain and wholesome. It could also be starchy and horrid. Once in every four or five Fridays I realised with a sinking heart that the meal was steamed fish. I could manage it as a rule except when it was cod – a full-sized fish, all of it, dumped on the serving-plate, head, tail and an eye that, dead and dreary though it was, seemed to be fixing me. I could never get the cod down. Its sauce, thin and watery with a bit of green parsley, did not help. All I could do was to sit, with tears trickling into the sauce, while I tried and tried to swallow a portion so large that I felt there must be some special spite against me. Now and then, if it was not too sloppy, I would sweep the whole thing into paper ready on my lap, roll it up, and push it into the elastic of my knickers to throw away later. That was the plan, but though I went prepared every time, I was not very clever and succeeded only once or twice. Failure was the end, for if you could not eat everything before you they would take it away, talking about the waste of God's food. Then at tea-time back it would be, the same old cod, cold now and jellied, and served to you by yourself at a side-table. Not that you were starved; they did allow you one piece of bread and a drink – cocoa usually – but no biscuit, no jam, no golden syrup.

Afterwards, if you still refused the cod, it disappeared. As far as I know, it returned only once; there were no refrigerators and it would not have been safe to keep it longer.

Some things I did look forward to: plum-duff particularly, with plenty of large sultanas; and on one Irish feast-day, colcannon, which meant cabbage and potato and onion fried up, rather like bubble-and-squeak, in a big enamel dish. It was a treat then; I loathe it now.

IV

My mother must have felt terrible about leaving me in such a place as an orphanage which was quite out of her class. She loved me; there was no question about that. With her dark hair, her long tailored brown suit with a jacket, and her rather nice blouses and gay hats, I was glad to think that she looked better than most of the mothers I saw. Her money struggles must have been bitter, for she had to keep herself besides paying whatever the nuns asked for me; naturally they wanted as much as they could. She had to provide my vests and underclothes, most things, in fact, except the uniform dress and pinafore, and it worried her desperately when I needed shoes; even if the nuns would get these, she had to pay for them herself.

Because on half-days from work she would have to see my father and do her shopping, she came to me only on Sundays, in a special sitting-room at the back of the orphanage. All high polish and carpet, it was quite unlike the other rooms I knew. I remember an old-fashioned musical-box, a large glass-fronted mahogany cabinet with a cylinder revolving inside. When you put a penny into this imposing piece of furniture, the box would play for you, very slowly, one of the long-drawn tunes popular in its time, 'Kathleen Mavourneen' probably, or 'I dreamt that I dwelt in marble halls'.

Though the musical-box excited me tremendously – a hint of the future, I daresay – I did not hear it very often. We had to be

quiet in the parlour where there were never more than four
people together. You met your mother here only if she could
pay something towards your keep, as mine did. Other girls went
into a much more informal room. I suppose that in a fashion
we were among the high society of the orphanage. Anyway, in
the parlour you sat quietly by your mother and she would give
you the fruit or whatever it was she had brought. The rather
grand persons my mother was working for then would often
send expensive chocolates for me, and, strangely, I felt rather
ashamed about it. Children never like to be different: I daresay I wanted to be just like the others.

It was all very difficult in the parlour; I could not talk freely
about myself. Instead, the nun would come round with a formal
report – 'Eily has been very happy,' 'Eily loves playing with the
other children' – and, as she spoke, I would be waiting anxiously
to know what my mother would say. I kept on prodding her
nervously which must have made the visit as much of an ordeal
for her as it was for me. In fact, we had no sort of understanding.
When I ought to have rushed into the room and hugged her, I
merely walked in self-consciously and gave her a kiss, the kind
of polite ceremony that really helped to estrange us. If we could
have gone off together on visiting days it would have been far
better, but probably the nuns thought a small child of six would
have been badly upset by any break with routine.

The rest of the children saw their parents in a room that was
reached by a separate door. Here they all sat happily on benches
at a long table; the parents would produce oranges or apples,
ordinary gifts, possibly a few sweets; and a nun would report
on anything special that might have happened to a child – other
than this, never interfering. I might not have known about this
room at all if a girl who was a friend of mine, Kathleen Doran,
had not taken me in to see her relatives at a time when my
mother could not come. It was exactly the reverse of the nearly
silent 'parlour' – you could hardly hear your own voice in the
chattering.

My mother would send me an occasional postcard, an Easter

card, of course, and at Christmas a book or a toy – never a letter.
I cannot remember any toys at the orphanage, not even building-
blocks except for a group of the very small girls. If you wanted
to play you had to use your imagination, though they did hand
out a few games on Sundays, snap cards or snakes-and-ladders,
besides battered old story-books. Many children liked to knit,
making horses' reins on cotton-reels. I had a doll of some kind,
but they let me have it only on Sundays, a day I enjoyed. Otherwise I played by the hour with paper dolls, cutting them out
and drawing faces on them.

V

While I was at the orphanage I was taken ill and they sent me
down from London to a branch in Dover where children stayed
during convalescence; a small house with not many of us in it,
so we were treated rather as a large family. My father, who was
a trifle better then and away from hospital, came to visit me; I
believe we spent the day together by the sea, and I can recall
now those awful moments at parting. I must have been heart-
broken when he left me: these genuinely emotional things stick
in my mind, and I know I had to be dragged away from him.
In any trouble at a big school you did feel absolutely alone. A
nun might say lightly, 'Oh, she'll be all right in a little while;
she'll have forgotten it,' but this was just a half-truth. You had
to get over it by yourself; the marks would remain, so would
that fearful sense of loneliness.

Once I was taken to see my father's hospital, an enormous
place it looked to me, where people were sitting about in groups
and my parents and myself were together. Clearly he was very
ill indeed and despondent; again I had this longing to stay with
him. When he died – and it was nothing to do with his breakdown, he died of pneumonia – I have no memory now of going
to his funeral or of being upset, just a dazed notion that I was
playing a part and had to keep looking sad for days at a time.

Something out of the ordinary had happened; suddenly everyone was nice to me, and sorry. From the mourning I wore, I
still think of a black beaver hat with a large brim; so big, black,
and furry that I can hardly forget it.

Quite another period was beginning. Now we had to be on
our own, my mother wrote to everyone in the family she knew,
asking for help to get me into a better school. A distant relative,
Lady Macdonald, agreed to pay for me at the Ursuline Convent
at Brentwood in Essex. That was an excitement because of the
long list of clothes I needed: two or three of everything – even
my own towels – and my first dressing-gown. The uniform was
to be a brown dress and coat, one for summer, another for
winter. All of this took time, but at last I was fitted out, my
new trunk was tightly packed, and I said a tearful goodbye to
Sister Frances, who was crying too. At the orphanage I had been
made to think of myself as a special person, slightly above some
of the others. My new convent life would be a most startling
change.

CHAPTER TWO

Convent Girl

MOST of the girls at the Ursuline Convent had parents and comfortable homes. Trying to compete with them and pretending that my own home was just as real and just as comfortable, I would lose myself in fantasy and tell what I suppose now were the most fabulous lies. Even then, I still felt inferior, though there were one or two compensations. After all, a maternal great-aunt was or had been a Reverend Mother at a similar convent in Ireland. Somewhere along the line, too, there was a Bishop I had never seen, probably a relative of Lady Macdonald, who would send me the odd ten shillings, in those days a lot of money. That gave me a big lift. Having to make the best of things I made, characteristically, three times as much.

It did not altogether work. Yet I could have been perfectly happy there if I had not felt so much poorer than the rest when I looked at the tennis court and the skating-rink – our convent was surprisingly modern – and the paths on which you could ride your bicycle, assuming that you had one. No luck for me. Only my bare school bills were paid, no extras at all; so I had neither skates, bicycle, nor tennis racquet. I might borrow another girl's skates now and again, or get a game of tennis, but to lend anyone a bicycle was firmly forbidden. Here I saw myself, rather dramatically, as a deprived child with a grievance. This aside, it was sheer grandeur to have a cubicle to myself for the first time; a wardrobe and a built-in cupboard, a bed with a coloured eiderdown, and a jug and basin on a smaller cupboard, with a mirror over them. A strip of carpet lined the dormitory, and I had a piece of it by my bed. There I could be apart and yet conscious of my friendly neighbours. Downstairs the refectory, even its cups and saucers, was pleasanter than at the orphanage. Here we had small, sunny classrooms and carpeted floors, no bare boards. A delightful place if I had not been, apparently, the one girl in it without home, stability, or background. This was the worst imaginable time for problems. As I would discover, the influence of your early years is lasting, and my experience at the convent would create the inner loneliness from which I have suffered all my life.

For that period, I think, our Reverend Mother must have been uncommonly advanced, though she was a snob into the bargain, a distant person who favoured the grander girls. Many of us hardly saw her. I did because, having a good voice, I was in the choir, and she liked to play the organ herself while we stood singing round her. In my last year I learned music and arranged somehow to slide into the dancing class. Really I enjoyed this more than anything else, and I enjoyed our own notion of the theatre – something that, remarkably, the Reverend Mother loved. We were lucky enough to have a big stage at the head of the Assembly Hall, and this must have had a bearing on my future: they thought then that I had a comic streak, and certainly I could be a good mimic. There was generally something to act. On Sunday evenings one class or another would do a play, for preference a 'safe' recognised comedy like Box and Cox. Oddly, no Shakespeare. I assume that he was safe to study, but not to act; in class we would go through any play of his that happened to be on the English syllabus for our Oxford exams – Prelim., Junior, or Senior – but that was all. Every Christmas we would put on a Nativity by one of the Sisters which involved a lot of singing: carols and hymns.

I am sure we were amateurish to a degree, but it was never less than fun: not much talent, any amount of enthusiasm. If a girl had to appear as a man, her version of trousers would be two bags tied with tape well above the knee. As the jacket, in

any event, had to be pretty long, she looked like nothing more
masculine than the Man in the Moon. All of us had fairly long
hair which had to be bunched up out of sight under whatever
hat the 'man' wore; if he was without one the hair was wound
tightly about the head and brushed flat. Instead of a play we
might sometimes have a programme of songs, duets, piano
pieces, perhaps the reading of a poem. A sister of one of our
nuns was, improbably, a professional whistler, and when she
came to us she obligingly did her turn. Also we had as a postulant a cousin (I think she was) of the humorist Jerome K.
Jerome: an amusing, talented young woman who would read
extracts from *Three Men In A Boat.*

Naturally we had hobbies. I spent hours drawing in pencil –
conventional sketches, trees precisely shaded, flowers and animals, but never people. Afterwards I would colour them from
one of the paintboxes that often turned up as birthday presents.
Also I read a great deal, the kind of books you might have expected: *The Scarlet Pimpernel,* Susan Coolidge's *What Katy
Did Next,* and so on in a mixture of the schoolgirlish and the
romantic. It could be a bit of a puzzle to organise your reading.
They handed out the books at a week-end and collected them
again; and obviously if you were in the middle of a story you
wanted to keep it back. That was not easy. Three of us, I remember, chose a book we could read and hide together. By day
an upstairs lavatory was as good as anywhere: you would go
in and read your chapter until a violent thumping on the door
warned you to let in the next tenant. At night it was harder;
we took turns to hide the book under a mattress or somewhere
else out of the way, but in the end, even in the great cause of
literature, it got too frustrating and we had to give it up.

Writing home was a regular chore. If letters addressed to us
were not opened we usually read them to the nun and never
felt that they were ours. Any letters we wrote ourselves we
left open for the Sister to read. There was also a special period
when we copied a letter from the blackboard – I suppose to
relieve the nuns who must have been weary of us sitting there,

elbows on the desk, wondering what on earth we could say. The formal piece had to begin with a few set phrases: 'Spring is coming; it is lovely to see the daffodils showing themselves,' or 'the dear little snowdrops'. In winter: 'Now the snow is on the ground and everything looks very beautiful.' In autumn something about the leaves and their beautiful tints – no letter without its scrap of natural history and its adjectives. Bits of information next: 'Sister Mary So-and-So is very ill, and we all said a prayer for her in the chapel; she is getting a little better.' Then the nun would chalk a large 'I' on the blackboard, and that would be the sign for us to write personally to dear Mummy or Daddy, Auntie or Uncle, to thank them for what they had said in their last letters, and to comment on it. Back after this to the form-letter: we were getting on well with our studies and must mention what we enjoyed most. The nun would turn to me:

'Now, Eileen, say how much you like your drawing, though this doesn't mean, of course, that you are neglecting your academic subjects. You expect to pass whatever exam you are taking.'

We all had to say that we were well, and that if we had a slight cold it was getting better, and Sister had been very good to us. Further, if Mother or Uncle or Granny were ill, we hoped they would be improving and we would say a prayer for them. We signed ourselves either 'With love' or 'Yours affectionately', and that was it. We were allowed to ask for more money. I never did; my mother had enough to do, as it was, to pay for any extras.

As no parent would read another's correspondence, all of this must have sounded quite convincing, certainly as dull as the usual boarding-school letter unless a girl was able to work in something on the sly. It could be done.

II

At my age the religious side of the convent affected me. I loved the Midnight Mass at Christmas: the feeling of going to church so late; the decorations and the lights; the carol-singing and the crib – again, I daresay, a theatrical impulse. First Communion had its special quality of holiness. The May processions excited me: the moment when, two by two and veiled in white, we walked from the church into the grounds. It was a privilege then to hold the strings of a banner. Those May hymns were cheerful: one of them, 'Bring flowers of the rarest, bring flowers of the fairest,' had a tune like a jig. A Dominican Father was visiting us once, and from the back of the church where I was standing with the choir, I could see him when the music began, jigging to it gaily until it was time for him to enter and pace solemnly up the nave. Really, at this period, I quite enjoyed religion. We had only a few hell-fire sermons, mostly during retreat. These impressed me for an hour or so and made me resolve never to lie again – a vow that, goodness knows, was needed; at the convent diplomatic lying was a part of my daily life.

Its Mass aside, I hated Christmas. Those of us, very few, who remained at the convent during the holidays were lonely and depressed. One year during the war four girls were there with me, two of them German and two Irish. Christmas Eve somehow was exciting; after Midnight Mass we had a kind of hot-punch fruit drink and cake. Next morning we stayed late in bed; we had a small tree, and our presents were given out after breakfast (mine were books and sweets, possibly a postal order and a box of paints). There was a good midday dinner, but one of the German girls was crying, none of us felt at all cheerful, and later for several hours the nuns left us alone. Though we read our books and tried dimly to amuse ourselves until tea at five or six, a faintly party-ish meal with extra cakes and biscuits, I remember being thoroughly miserable. After tea they left us again until bedtime.

B

Curiously I had liked Christmas at the orphanage. We were all together as usual. On Christmas Eve we hung our stockings expectantly at the foot of the bed; next morning, when we woke slightly earlier, it was a joy to sit up and rummage, to find a sugar mouse, a few inexpensive toys, some biscuits and an orange. Not much, but we were happy, and the nuns were happy too. They had hung coloured paper chains in the refectory, dinner and tea were feasts, we had a cracker each, and we were never left alone. I was young, of course; older girls might not have had the fun of the stocking. All the same, it would be a cheerful day for everybody; even the devotional side was brighter, and we sang carols beside the crib. At the Ursuline Convent the nuns would simply hand on to us their Christmas duties and leave it at that. No warmth or jollity – I hated it. My mother was obliged to stay at her work, though if they knew she had a child at school, her employers might send me chocolates in a fancy box.

Holidays, on the whole, I dreaded. Not long before the end of term every girl who was going home had her trunk brought from the store-room and planted at the end of her bed. They would be hilarious and excited as they packed their things. I seldom went home, only in one or two summers when my mother gave up her job for a while so that I could stay with her in rooms, always rooms. About every third Saturday we moved. Two weekends might be peaceful, but at the third there we were again, traipsing round, searching for a better bargain and a woman who was not 'robbing' us. If we were not changing rooms, the furniture had to be shifted, the bed put at another angle, and the sideboard in the middle of the room or under a window.

It was the dreariest time: those summer holidays, many weeks of them, seemed unending. Occasionally other girls asked me to join them, but I did not like this either, having so little to wear – my school uniform and possibly a couple of dresses – and knowing that I must have appeared gauche. My mother must have been just as worried. She had to think of changing any uniform I had grown out of and getting a dressmaker to follow the regulation pattern. For me this calling on a dress-maker and shopping for materials would be the best things in a holiday: outings to be followed by tea and cakes in a shop.

A few cotton frocks were run up for me in the summer, though (except when a girl at school invited me for a week) I was never at the seaside. I feared to be asked out. Even the idea that I might bump into a convent girl in the street bothered me – not that one would be likely to turn up in Hammersmith or Fulham, they were scattered right across England. I was friendly with Daphne Josephs, younger of two sisters in a rich Jewish family who spent their winters at the Hotel Cecil in the Strand, where Shell-Mex House is now; in the summers they travelled. Daphne was constantly asking me to tea, or to stay with her in the holidays. When I did go to tea I felt shy and awkward. Kind though they were, buying a huge box of choco-lates and sending me back in a cab, I used to return with tears in my eyes and quite sure that I must be looking awful.

I began to be obsessed with a passion for nice things. One holiday I noticed in a second-hand shop some splendidly laun-dered lacy underclothes: two pairs of knickers and two night-dresses with beautifully cut yokes, long sleeves, and more lace on their cuffs. After gazing and gazing whenever I passed the shop, I went in boldly one morning and paid the woman what for me was a fortune, ten shillings on account. Between them the garments cost thirty shillings; she promised she would keep them for me, and in some way I scraped the rest of the money together. Transported with delight – and that is no exaggeration – I took the things home to pack away safely in my school luggage.

III

That was a bewildering time. My mother had the old-fashioned belief that a child and her mother must love each other as a matter of course. I was searching all the while for the kind of true security and home life I could talk about at school without feeling self-conscious. We had little money; in any event, my mother was hardly the type to take me out to the pictures – or anywhere else. Ironically, I would be glad to get to school again and see my special friends there, even if I felt absurdly apart when they were talking of the places they had been to and what they had done. More than anything I longed for the solid foundation these other girls had; I could merely listen to them or invent incredible tales about my own holiday.

At home I had been more insecure than ever. 'How am I going to pay for your uniform?' my mother would sigh. 'Surely you haven't outgrown your shoes again? . . . Really, Eileen, you're growing enormously!' With the cuffs of my school mac and overcoat disappearing up my arms, I might have been a gorilla. My coat was invariably tight: after the first days at home I knew that I was the biggest girl in town. Moreover, I had a lot of hair, very thick, and my uniform hat had a way of sitting on it like a small pot. The convent did a brisk trade with its badges, including an elaborate one, silver and blue, for fixing in the middle of the hatband; when I needed a new hat – this was every term, my head seemed to grow so rapidly – the nuns had a marvellous habit of charging for a new badge, and my poor mother must have bought fourteen or fifteen of them. My gloves, which never fitted me, were the same that Lady Macdonald had bought when I left the orphanage. Good ones, I kept them until they barely reached my wrists. Still, even then they had their uses, for if I took them off somebody was bound to say to my mother, 'Your child has lovely hands, Mrs Reynolds. I thought when she was sitting with her gloves on that there was something wrong . . . they looked slightly deformed.' On the whole, I was scarcely an imposing picture in my teenage years: bursting out of my coat, a felt hat perched on my head, and gloves that were probably five sizes too small.

I must have been looking like this when I was out with my mother in Walham Green Market early in August 1914. We were both fond of the market, in the evening especially, its naphtha lights kindled like gigantic flares – you wondered if the whole place might go up in fire at any moment. There was such a sense of gaiety as you walked round its stalls. Those Cockneys who sold corn-cures or cough medicine or ointment for rheumatism were music-hall acts in themselves, quite tireless in patter and energy. To prove his miracles the corn-curer displayed a 'perfect' foot. On the rheumatism poster a man twisted in agony was ready at a touch of the ointment to be lithe and pain-free. The weight-reducer showed an enormous woman who took the right medicine and dwindled to a sylph (my cue perhaps).

There, among the market-stalls, we heard that England was at war. Doubly worried, about her own work as well as getting me off to school, my mother immediately returned to our rooms to pack. The convent, we found, had booked a special train, and next day I went across to Liverpool Street Station where some of the girls had met for the journey to Brentwood. The air tingled with expectation. We arrived to find that the army had commandeered part of the convent; rows of soldiers with their boots off were sitting in the skating-rink, having their feet examined. Some, who had been marching for miles, were town boys who had never taken much exercise, certainly had never route-marched.

For the next three weeks soldiers drilled in the rink and in the playground next to it. Their side of the convent was separate from ours, but we watched excitedly from the corridor windows and if a man glanced up to wave or wink at us, a few of the girls would get giggly and hysterical. It was soon over. Our nuns were prudent enough to let us into the corridor only when the men were away; at other times one or two of the girls who had developed rapid 'crushes' had to sneak in when they could. Presently they had nothing at all to see. The men, who had been brought to the convent in an emergency, were dispersed now to other billets.

During the war we hardly gathered what was happening. Children must have done who had fathers in the army or navy; I had no father and cannot even recall now much that was said (so unlike the Second War when I had a job to do). Convent food may have been scantier; it was not noticeably bad – we kept chickens and grew our own vegetables. Possibly clothes rationing affected our uniforms. Blinds were pulled down in the dormitory, but nothing compared with the stringent black-out of the 1940s. Hazily – I must have been on holiday with my mother in London – I recall a Zeppelin overhead. Nothing else; no horrors. The war had to be remote until I was older, and men who had been in the trenches and lived through a sustained misery would tell me their stories of Flanders.

Even if I had pretended to giggle with the other girls, those troops at the convent had not greatly stirred me. But I was crazy about one of our Sisters. A few of us, suffering from adolescent crushes, would hurry to open the door when she was passing; if she was on duty at recreation we sat adoringly; if it was in the outside playground we collected around her. Some of the nuns would never allow their 'pets' to talk to them. My favourite was soft-hearted; only three or four of us competed to be near her, and though she made us go off now and again to play with the rest, she would also talk for moments that were dazzling to remember. Undoubtedly (I was twelve or thirteen) I was almost in love with her and cherished every word she spoke. She was my dormitory Sister. Once a week she brushed my hair; long and thick, it had to be plaited tightly for six days in seven, but on Sundays I could wear it loose in a band.

Sister Margaret Mary's weekly brushing was an hour for day-dreams. I never thought of boys in mine. Instead I looked ravishing and did something out of the ordinary – probably singing at a great concert with crowds of people clapping and always Sister Margaret Mary to admire me and applaud.

IV

The convent's cleaning and dusting were left to its lay sisters who did all our mending as well. When our bed-linen was

changed even the clean sheets were put on for us, though for
the rest of the week we made the beds ourselves. It was poor
training. On leaving school we instinctively expected someone
else to do the domestic work.

After some time I was proud to get a privileged job, helping
a nun in the chapel with the flowers and Sanctuary lamps. Any
worn-down candles had to be changed. Those used for Feast
Days, Sundays and Benedictions were particularly precious;
made of special wax, they had been blessed and were set in fine
silver or brass containers. Hence a minor tragedy: I could not
have thought about it as minor at the time. In my last year
half a dozen of us planned a midnight dormitory feast which
sounds now like a chapter from Enid Blyton or Angela Brazil. A
few weekly boarders were to bring what they could; we others had
the pocket-money we spent as a rule on Saturdays at the school
shop (sweets, flannels, soap, toothbrushes, medals and so on). In
one way and another we collected enough for the feast: buns
and biscuits, lemonade, chocolates. It took us days to assemble
the stuff and to hide it. On the night, when the dormitory went
dark about nine-thirty, I was to bring the used candles from the
chapel, and somehow I managed to do this without being
spotted. My own cubicle was farthest from the Sister-in-charge
who slept in the next dormitory, so we met there, lit the
candles and began to eat. No good; we must have been careless.
The nun woke, she discovered us in the midst of the orgy, and
next day you might have thought that Eileen Reynolds had
robbed a bank. It was not so much the food. I had taken the
chapel candles and one of these had been blessed. It was sacri-
lege.

'You must be expelled,' said the Reverend Mother.

She spoke too quickly, for I had no home to go to; my mother
lived at her work. (I heard afterwards that she received a letter
reporting my crime.) What could be done? Since no one must
let me contaminate others, the sentence was exile to a small
branch school, for the youngest children, in the neighbouring
village of Billericay. At first I was rather pleased, for my adored

Sister Margaret Mary had gone for a term to the same school.
But when I got to it and missed friends of my own age, I was
just bored, lonely and lost. Worse, Sister Margaret Mary had
returned to the convent.

My mother could not leave her work, and it would not have
helped if she had; we were too far apart. Studying was a trial.
I began to feel ill and even to walk in my sleep, yet nobody
worried; for most of the time they left me to myself, a forgotten
number, and I had to fill in the days looking after the small
ones. It could hardly have been a bigger relief when the penance
ended. Back with my friends in the convent, it was as if I had
been absent for a term on holiday.

During an official holiday I had nowhere to go, and several
weeks to get through; some younger girls were also marooned
with me. Then Reverend Mother had an idea. The widowed
father of two Irish girls, about six and seven, had rented a house
in the district so that he could have them with him at week-
ends. Surely I might go to Mr O'Reilly's by day and return to
the convent at night? Fond of the pair and ready to enjoy myself, I went off to the first week-end. It was anything but enjoyable. Sending the girls to play on their own, Mr O'Reilly
spent the whole time fondling me. I had no idea how to cope
with him. I did not like the man, had no notion of what
it was all about, and could not repel him entirely. Every week-
end, every second he could have me alone, the annoyance continued. Uneasy and self-conscious, I spent nerve-straining hours
trying to play with the children and escape from their father.

The convent was unsympathetic. When I said after the first
visit that I would rather not go again – and I said it as strongly
as I could – Reverend Mother told me I was silly and ungrateful.
What did I object to? Wasn't it a holiday every week? I had
no means of explaining, and the agony went on for two or
three more week-ends until I flatly refused to go back. Here I
began to sob. Reverend Mother said curtly, 'You must be absolutely stupid!' Not alarming in itself, I daresay. But, brought
up as I had been, it frightened me. Clearly I must be to blame

for something no one ever discussed: a mystery, an unknown horror. I had never heard the word 'sex'. Today no adolescent girl or boy could have suffered like this, yet neither my mother nor the nuns would have dreamt of mentioning the subject.

V

My last term was chaotic. I started to sleepwalk again, and to have mild fits in my sleep. Morning by morning I woke with a bad headache, and sometimes my tongue would be swollen where I had bitten it. This, too, while I was studying for the Oxford Senior exam; eventually I must have struggled through the questions and grazed through on the lowest possible pass.

That summer I was going home. Though I seemed to be dazed rather than ill, my appearance shocked my mother when she met me at Liverpool Street Station. Once more I had attacks during the night; the doctor said we must consult a nerve specialist, and he told us why I had broken down: a perfectly normal cause, the stoppage of my periods. I had not mentioned it to the nuns because in our code it was another thing entirely secret and personal, definitely not talked about. My mother was sure that I had inherited something from my father and must be going slightly mad. (He had been simply a victim of extreme depression; as I have said, even in those unenlightened days he was never certified.)

Deep within her, my mother, as a semi-trained nurse, must surely have guessed what was wrong with me. That would have been too simple; temperamentally, she had to be sorry for herself, to imagine me a fearful burden, to dramatise me as likely to go off my head. At length I was to enter a nursing home. When the arrangement had been made she resumed her work and told them at the convent that I would not be coming back to Brentwood. So the final break was sudden and complete: no goodbye to the girls or to the nuns. I had left school for ever.

CHAPTER THREE

On My Own

ORPHANAGE to convent, convent to nursing home: I was seeing life. The home, or sanatorium, I was sent to in Brighton was an agreeable place, soundly managed, with several private rooms and two larger rooms, six or seven beds in each. I was in a larger room, lucky to have the company of girls from a neighbouring school, Roedean. Treatment was not very strenuous: baths principally, a strict diet, and, I suppose, necessary drugs. Soon I was much better. We had a common-room with a piano that one of the girls played confidently, so I would sing a great many songs and imagine myself in opera. One afternoon, while I was on the front with my new friends, I saw Sister Margaret Mary and another nun, her superior, walking towards us. I raced over to Sister who was about to greet me when her companion checked her, asked me frigidly how I was, and drew her away. It was so devastating that I have never forgotten. I could only guess that either my mother had written in alarm and told them that they had ruined my health, or else, more plainly, that Eileen Reynolds was the poor girl of the school and the nun's attitude was wholly snobbish. If it seems trivial now, it war far from trivial then.

After I had been at the home for a time the doctor said that I was physically well, but for the sake of my nerves I must stay as much as possible in the open air. Without money I had to work. The woman doctor suggested gardening. She knew a big house near Burgess Hill where they would train a young girl while giving her pocket-money and her keep. I went there. The

owners, a curious couple, had a head gardener and a younger
one besides myself, and a pair of monkeys that frightened me
and had the run of the place unchecked. Dressed suitably in
overalls, I seemed to be at it morning to night, weeding the
beds or edging the grass, jobs I loathed. The days lingered on;
sometimes I ate with the family, sometimes in the kitchen. It
was simply a dead end.

In those days I was still practising my religion. On my few
week-ends at the house, I went on Sundays to the nearest
church, a convent chapel in Burgess Hill. When the Reverend
Mother invited me to breakfast and a talk after Mass, she heard
my troubles and thought she might solve them. Why didn't I
work, she said, in the convent grounds, a vast stretch with its
acreage of lawns and vegetable gardens, and its greenhouses for
flowers, fruit, and tomatoes? I was surprised when she told me
it was a home for rich mental patients – by now everyone
seemed to have decided that I must be half-mad myself. They
gave me a bedroom with my own bathroom. A young lay sister
helped a little in the garden and the greenhouses, and there
were two young boys. Generally I had to pick flowers for the
patients' rooms which were either luxurious suites or com-
munal quarters for the less well off. Flowers apart, I spent the
day in picking ripe tomatoes, boxing bunches of grapes, and
packing the peaches carefully in cotton-wool. On wet days, with
not much to do outside, I helped a warm and lively young nun
to sort the linen. She was my saving grace. Probably I had the
usual crush on her; I would put the linen purposely into the
wrong piles, realising that after she had got into a temper, her
hugs and kisses would give me the affection I had missed.
Neither of the two garden-boys was attractive, one simple, the
other stone-deaf. Though the head gardener flirted gently and
said how pretty I looked, he was never any sort of problem.

In those days I was terrified to be alone in my room at night,
fearing that heaven knows what might creep from behind the
curtain. On my weekly half-day I would go to Brighton with
some of the convent maids. If, by any chance, I came back

alone, the walk from the station at dusk down a long lane would scare me into running like mad from an unknown pursuer, banging the convent gate, and looking back to see merely leaves and pieces of paper blowing and scuffling after me in the gloom.

My nerves were not soothed yet. But I had an unexpected delight: a meeting with the engraver, artist and stone-cutter, Eric Gill. Walking one afternoon, I began to chat to a thin, ascetic-looking man who asked me to his 'colony' on Ditchling Common, not far from the convent; he must have seen I was lonely, for he told me to come back whenever I wished. It was a place where different groups of colonists made their own clothes from homespun wool – in the circumstances they could hardly be fashion-plates – knitted their socks, made their own shoes, even used plates from their own pottery, and if possible (though not wholly vegetarian) ate only things from the earth. Nuts, raisins, vegetable dishes: today we should call it health food. Many people lived there, families of them, so I did not feel out of it. All I had ever done before had been highly conventional. I found now a fresh simplicity and strength, a good taste I had never experienced. One of the nuns told me later that Eric Gill was a little eccentric; certainly I would never have thought it.

II

My mother, who was nurse-companion then to a Miss Kay at the village of Wivelsfield Green, also in Sussex, had decided to rest in London for a time. I might as well fill her place, she said; no duties except companionship. It was a small, plain, comfortable cottage. Its owner looked after us; Miss Kay herself, odd in appearance, morose and silent, was slightly unhinged, if not certifiable. For me that was a familiar story – I wondered if I should ever escape from it. Yet quite soon I did. Miss Kay's brother, shocked to see such a young girl in charge, moved her up to a small London residential hotel where my mother, who was lodging then near World's End, Chelsea, could visit her every day and shop for her. I returned to London also. The problem was how to earn a living. After all my expensive education I was good at two things: I could sing and dance.

After a few weeks Miss Kay decided she must go back to the country. My mother, with the small pension she had from my father's employers, announced that she was no longer fit for work. It was up to me to help to keep us both, and from that time until her death forty years later, I gave money to her every week – money that, after our marriage, Sean provided.

At first I thought of tracing and settled down to learn it at the Polytechnic's night classes in architectural drawing. Meantime, having to get a job to tide us over, I got several, very mixed. None of them lasted. Thus, from a 'Wanted' advertisement, they took me on in a shoe-shop, and most charming I was with the customers; when the social part was over and I was left with piles of shoes to put away, I muddled boxes, shoes, and sizes so hopelessly that after a week the manager paid me off in despair. Christmas was near. Engaged as an assistant in the handbag department of a shop in St Paul's Churchyard, I found that I was selling the bags without trouble, making commission besides my wages, and getting along well with the other girls who were friendly and young. At lunch with one of them – it was generally coffee and sandwiches in a restaurant round the corner – I heard the waitress exclaim, 'Eileen! Whatever are you doing here!' Looking up, I saw the young postulant, Jerome's relation, who had been at the convent and must have left it before she was professed. Promptly she gave me two cakes for the price of one, and at every lunch-hour I had all the pies and pastries I needed – no worries about slimming. The handbag job over, I never saw my postulant friend again.

Where next? After my Polytechnic classes I had nerve enough to go to the Architects' Association; they might help me, I argued, to work as a tracer. Aware by now that I was attractive to men I told my tale with all the dramatic force I knew: my poor mother, my problems in looking after her, my dire need of work. At the convent I had had years of experience in tall stories; it was second nature, and I could be so persuasive and sad-eyed that I almost believed myself (an excellent test). The Architects' Association believed me. Sympathetically, they sent me to temporary jobs at various offices, and in the end I reached the big pottery firm of Doultons at Lambeth. Captain Corby, its head, employed me as a tracer of wash-basins, baths, lavatory plans, and so forth, sometimes a complete bathroom. He liked me, often took me to lunch, and grew into a steady friend.

III

Life with my mother was progressively trying. We had no ideas in common; she simply thought of getting money week by week. Also, to my anger, she had started to drink. (Thanks to the convent, I was a thorough prude.) Not a constant drinker, there were periods when she had to have it; I loathed the smell of stout which was all she could afford, and instead of seeing she was ill – for compulsive drinking is an illness – looked upon it sternly as a disgrace to us both. On recovering from these fits she would feel sick, go to bed and send for the doctor, and if I were going out she would cry and say how dreadful it was for a child to leave her mother. I hated it, but convent training can make one submissive – a mixture of submission and revolt. At last I had to rebel in earnest. When she pawned one of my dresses I threatened to leave her, and this did genuinely frighten her, though at heart I knew that if she were really ill I would never have the courage to clear off. Once, longing to go out, I asked the doctor if she could be left. He laughed at me: 'But surely you don't stay in? There's nothing wrong with her.'

We had been writing letters to anybody who might help. One went to Lady Macdonald, and I imagine she must have provided the introduction to a Mrs Jones, a wealthy woman, kind, and interested in music. Hearing I dreamt of being a singer, she arranged a voice-test with a distinguished teacher at the Aeolian

Hall, Mr de Lisle, and later paid for my lessons with him.
Naturally my failures to practise annoyed him – but how could
I have been conscientious? I had no piano, and I was at work
all day. Mrs Jones gave me some clothes – I was destined to be
in debt to the rich – and I was sent also to a Lady Parsons who
lived in a large Brook Street house full of servants. Meeting her
really changed the course of my life. She introduced me to a
professional pianist who took after-dinner engagements, sometimes with a violinist, a cellist, and a singer; and for concerts
in the big Brook Street drawing-room I received a guinea (the
pianist had two) as well as my dinner. We ate this in what
might have been the breakfast-room; later we could either go
home or return to the guests. Preferring once or twice to return,
I met the then Home Secretary, Edward Shortt, who was most
courteous. I did sense a real change in myself. I had had my
hair bobbed – something that in my eyes made me a new person
with a new personality – and my clothes were becoming; when
Mrs Jones gave any of her daughter's dresses to me she took
care to have them altered by a good dressmaker.

Next I answered an advertisement for a concert-party singer.
This proved to be for a pierrot troupe, eight of us in traditional
pom-poms, who performed in the evenings and on Saturdays on
the outskirts of London. (We opened the show with 'How 'ya
gonna keep 'em down on the farm, after they've seen Paree?')
The engagement faded away after three weeks, but I fell in love
with one of the two men who ran the troupe, a baritone singer
named Bert Elen, nephew of Gus Elen, the music-hall comedian.
His brother Alec, a wild type, had got into trouble and been
imprisoned; and Bert, who was sure the sentence was mistaken,
begged me to speak to Edward Shortt. It needed a lot of courage.
Still I telephoned Mr Shortt who received me in his Whitehall
office, discussed the case carefully, and did get the sentence
reduced.

The same brother Alec had a girl friend, a schizophrenic;
when they persuaded me to go round to her for a few hours a
day I felt doomed once more to be with the mentally deranged.

A pleasant girl, she quickly grew worse and had to be put into a home where I visited her; normal as a rule, she was convinced she had contracted syphilis which had affected her brain. Looking after her was a way of earning a few pounds. I did her shopping and kept her company, and astonishingly my mother never asked me about it.

In other matters she asked too much. Bert often took me out; we would kiss each other romantically, and when I got home my mother would call me depraved. 'Out till all hours!' she would say, prodding me suspiciously. 'What have you been up to?' Nothing dreadful except the hugging and the lingering kisses. But Bert was not a Catholic; I still attended Mass and confession, and any prospect of a mixed marriage was impossible. My mother was urgently against it; I had a tearful parting and wept for days. Then I met a Civil Servant from Lincoln, aged twenty-seven and quiet, younger than Bert and not in the least like him. Again I believed that this was love. Every Saturday we walked either to Hendon or into the Buckinghamshire country to have tea at a village shop; kissing and cuddling went on for ages, and it bored me sometimes. I must have been quite wrong for a good, steady, and extremely serious lad from Lincoln. At heart I knew what I really wanted, and he understood that I was having singing lessons and hoped to go on the stage. My mother appreciated him – he used to take her to tea at a Lyons Corner House – but there was no conceivable future. He, too, was not a Roman Catholic, so I had as usual to break it off, with the inevitable pangs. He wrote me long letters. I wrote to him. 'How can we part?' we said. But we did.

I ought to be fair to my mother. However possessive she might be (and she was), she always cooked my meals and never expected me to do much in the house, never any floor-scrubbing or rough work; our landlady cleaned the rooms once a week and washed the sheets and tablecloths. My best clothes I looked after myself, with reverent care.

That said, life at home was a steady trial. Between her spells of drinking my mother would get extra religious, and honestly

I wonder now which was worse. With other people she was far better and gayer; alone we just could not mix. I was a lively girl, laughing and mimicking; though very occasionally she would laugh with me, mostly she nagged, and it was then that my rebellious, independent side took charge. One day, since the job with Doultons appeared to be permanent, I vowed to myself that I would leave home and get my own room. This must be the final break.

The room I rented was tiny but cheerful enough, an attic at the top of a house in north-west London – Goldhurst Terrace near Swiss Cottage. It had barely anything in it: a bed, a chair, a small table, a gas-ring, and a food cupboard. The landlady, a motherly person in the right sense, brought cups, saucers and plates, a kettle and a little saucepan; I had a chest of drawers and a curtain behind which I hung my clothes. That was all I needed. It was like heaven. My only shopping was for corn-flakes, shredded wheat, and milk. I never troubled to boil an egg, to buy marmalade, or even to get a cup of tea. Captain Corby often invited me to meals, and I had several other friends.

For some days I was at peace there, but I could not have expected to be for long. My mother believed that I had been sent up to Stoke-on-Trent, a town that must have occurred to me because the pottery came from it and it was on the Doulton labels. To get money to her every week I had fixed up something ridiculously complicated with the Stoke-on-Trent post office. No good: I was a clumsy conspirator. After the first week I forgot where I ought to be and posted a letter from London; promptly my mother inquired about me, discovered my address, and bore down on Swiss Cottage. One evening I discovered her waiting in the hall after telling the landlady her long and tear-ful tale. Beside myself and resolved not to slip back, I climbed up to my room with her and had a frightful row on the spot. She was weeping. I was wretched. I had not left home with a flourish to go off with a man. It was simply a desperate effort to be myself, and I thought it was understandable. Duty,

nothing else, had kept me with her; she interpreted duty in her
own way, believing that I must be responsible for her during the
rest of my life.

When she went that evening I expected that the landlady,
who had heard about my cruelty and wickedness, would tell me
to go as well. Actually she made some tea, talked sensibly for
a time, and gradually calmed me down. Nevertheless, I could
scarcely remain in Goldhurst Terrace, so what next? Through
Lady Macdonald I had met a Catholic canon whose church was
in the City and he invited me to talk to him if I had any problem. Now he recommended a ladies' club called Nutford House
in Seymour Street, Marble Arch. He coped with the excellent
references they needed, and my next months were almost peaceful. I met my mother, gave her what money I could, and left it
at that. Life was full; I continued my singing lessons, and Lady
Parsons helped me to another job. I ought, she suggested, to see
an acquaintance, Sir Woodman Burbidge, of Harrods: until I
found a way of using my voice, I might get something more
congenial than tracing 'bathroom accessories'. Sir Woodman
duly interviewed me. I recited my story, and the poor man
must have asked what in the name of goodness he could do.
Wisely, I had taken along my tracings. He sent me with them
to the head of Harrods' drawing and architectural office, and
very soon I was at work there. A boring job, it turned out to
be: mostly going into the main store with a man who measured
showcases and counters while I stood by with his parapher-
nalia. As soon as a plan for this or the other was fixed I could
get on with the tracing.

It was a small office: three draughtsmen, a senior man, and
a young one who was serving his time before he became an
architect. I was nothing but the odd body Sir Woodman had
had to fit in, but I did get what was important to me, a weekly
wage. During a lull I had to be shifted elsewhere. Another
Harrods man interviewed me, and, to put it plainly, I was employed to spy upon the shop assistants. Given an account in a
fictitious name, I would go shopping and would have then to

describe how various assistants had served me, whether they
were polite or cool, quick or slow. None of the goods I ordered
ever reached me except the perishables – flowers or food –
though I could keep any material or ribbon under one yard. The
food did help our evening meal at Nutford House, but I detested the job and willingly gave it up before I need have done.
Luckily the drawing-office had another burst of work so I was
not unemployed; unobtrusively I slid back to my tracing.

IV

Three of the Nutford House girls were to mean a lot to me.
Alison Duncan and her sister Isabel, who shared a large room,
had recently lost their parents; they were Scots, fairly well off.
Isabel, the elder, was a business man's secretary; I became even
friendlier with Alison, attractive, red-haired and about nineteen,
who was not at work. In entire seriousness I passed on my
singing lessons to her. That is, I hired the same studio and in-
structed her in what I had just learned. She insisted on paying
a small fee. How she was taught is anybody's guess, but she
did practise diligently and got so far as singing a number with
her voice well to the front and resonance at the back of the nose.

A third girl, Stella Greer, who lived next to me, was a
Canadian and a relative of the actor Raymond Massey. After an
affair with a working man her parents thought wholly un-
suitable, she came over to London and did various catalogue
sketches – children's clothes principally – for an advertising
agency in Holborn. Because both of us were short of money we
agreed to pool what we had and to share a room. Stella introduced me to a relative, Colonel Esme Berkeley, who began to
entertain me at such places as the Savoy and at sedate dinner-
dances where I was always presentable in evening dresses from
Mrs Jones. Stella was violently in love with Esme's wealthy
twin brother Roland, head of an American bank, with a house
in Chester Square. But owing to her habit of arriving in the

most ghastly 'artistic' creations, Roland had to avoid Esme's haunts and took her instead to such restaurants as the Lyons Popular in Piccadilly or the Trocadero.

In the summer of 1923, when I was still ambitious to go on the stage, my singing teacher, then a Miss Louise Trenton, got me a card for a Savoy Theatre audition. They were rare, for the D'Oyly Carte Opera Company, which did nothing but the chain of Gilbert and Sullivan operettas, seldom needed to recruit, and there were jobs for only two or three girls. My friends at Nutford House were as excited as I was. I practised my songs over and over. On the day, instead of going in to Harrods, I spent the morning putting things on and taking them off. I used little make-up or powder, just lipstick for a Cupid's bow; having good eyelashes, I never needed mascara. It was important in those days to have your hair correctly styled, and mine was bobbed and laid rather close to the face.

Alison had exquisite clothes, so I borrowed one of her dresses and Isabel's fur coat in a beautiful modern cut. That afternoon Stella, in cape and big Cavalier hat, was waiting at the Savoy to give me a bunch of violets. Inside the theatre nothing went wrong. They engaged me under my name of Eileen Reynolds; and Rupert D'Oyly Carte's wife, Lady Dorothy, a stately, handsome woman who had been listening from the stalls, asked me to come down to talk to her. She drove me back to her Mayfair flat in Derby Street and I was entirely willing to prattle on about what I hoped to do, and why.

Rehearsals for the autumn tour would begin in September; there was a month to wait. Triumphant, I returned from Lady Dorothy's to an anti-climax at Nutford House. When I told the head that I was going on the stage she replied sadly that I would have to leave as their rules forbade them to have anyone in the theatrical profession. Without knowing it, I had changed within an afternoon to a 'rogue and vagabond'.

CHAPTER FOUR

Touring in England

AGAIN I was searching for a room, this time not alone. When Stella said that she would leave Nutford House and join me, we answered a host of advertisements before choosing a bed-sitter at the top of a house in Chelsea. It had a gas stove on the landing and there was even a battered piano, a bonus for me as with my first stage job coming up, I was more anxious than ever about singing practice. Our landlord was a dentist. We saw soon enough why his pretty wife was jealous – he tried to grab a kiss whenever he could catch me on the stairs. Sydney Street was exhilarating in its way. A number of students had digs there, and some university boys on a top floor across the road would fling open their windows on a fine Saturday afternoon and call us over for a cup of tea. Esme and Captain Corby continued to take me out, and Stella had her Roland. She also had her job, so between us there was enough to eat.

The men I was with now were father-figures. Esme went on loving a woman he had expected to marry but who had gone instead to a 'jam and pickles' business man. He was always gallant, and we looked forward to our meetings, though I knew I was not dangerously in love. I daresay I enjoyed being spoilt by a man I liked; he could never have met a girl less sophisticated. Often he took round his niece who was a professional model; it was more than forty years before I met her, and that was after his death when she brought a jade box of Esme's I had long admired and he wished me to have.

While waiting anxiously for D'Oyly Carte rehearsals to begin

I developed throat trouble. The management sent me immediately to a specialist, Geoffrey Carte, who told me that I must have my tonsils out: hardly a major operation, but the news alarmed me – I felt sure that I was going to die. In spite of all this, however, I fell for Geoffrey Carte, who made the right benevolent fuss, putting me in a corner of the ward and seeing that I had special treatment. I survived; and soon I was well enough to have my first trip abroad, though not very far. Louise Trenton, my singing teacher, had planned to go with some of her pupils to Brittany; she knew a *pension* near St Malo where we could combine a fortnight's holiday with singing tuition, and Mrs Jones and some other friends clubbed together to pay for me.

Everything was fresh. At St Malo I enjoyed talking over coffee or soft drinks under the café awnings in the central square. On Sundays a big cinema screen went up in the open, and crowds would sit about watching the film and waiting for music through a loud-speaker. Anyone could dance to it, and everyone of any shape or size did. Our *pension* must have been half an hour away by tram. It was sunny and hot on the long sandy Breton beaches, and though I had never learned to swim I managed now to do a few strokes and to float. One moment was really grim and might have been grimmer. Floating on my back, I got out of my depth, sensed that I was going under, and panicked; somebody spotted me, and I was dragged, just conscious, to shore. I must have been nearly gone; they pulled up my arms to drain the water out of me and carried me back to the house where I slept and slept. Next day, frightened as I was, they told me to go back, if only to dabble in the shallows. It took me an age to throw off the shock. Even now I have to stop at about eight strokes, though I love the sea and will stay in it long after the good swimmers, the long-distance crowd, have had their time and come out.

In the morning we had our singing lessons; the rest of the day was ours. It was here that I met Helen Seldon, as she was then, who would be so loyal a friend. Most of us had good voices. Helen had not, but she was lonely and Miss Trenton, I believe, had asked her so that she could mix with girls of her own age. For all my strange childhood I was much more relaxed than Helen was, far more of an extrovert. When very young she had lost a much-loved mother; now, until she was twenty-one, she was living as a Ward in Chancery with a guardian (from the Napier-Clavering family) in Cavendish Square. The first rich person I knew intimately, she could persuade you that, while she was happy to give, you had even more to offer her. Certainly she showed me that money and the security that accompanied it were not everything. Helen made this Breton holiday for all of us; without her quiet generosity we should have missed a great deal.

II

Back in London I had to rush off to the D'Oyly Carte. The company, which was probably the most popular then touring, had already set out; I joined it, with a shocking cold, at Wolverhampton in October. Three of us were new and we travelled together from London, thawing slowly and telling each other a little about ourselves. Though the other girls were sharing digs, I had (a little grandly) booked a room of my own, chosen from the management's list. Not a particularly good choice. My landlady was kind in a homely way, but her tiny ground-floor room was part of a conservatory, unbearably humid: I had to be kept as hot as the plants, splendid for them, disastrous for my cold. Moreover, you had to go down a long garden path to an outside lavatory, no fun when it was raining, and in Wolverhampton it rained most of the time. By the back door the landlady kept a big umbrella. She could have added gum-boots and a mackintosh.

We were to start rehearsing on the day after we arrived. I reported with no voice at all; no one could hear my name, much less my singing, so I had to sit glumly, mouthing the words. Wolverhampton that fortnight seemed deadly; not a boy-friend

in sight. Only Captain Corby was interested enough to travel
up. It would never have occurred to Esme, and if it had the place
would have horrified him. In future, I decided, I would share
with the other girls; cheaper for all of us and friendlier when
going home at night.

Stage make-up was the next question. I hadn't a clue. I had
never been to an acting school, and in private life I made up
very little. Now here I was, faced by a large and important-look-
ing tin box with spaces for numbered sticks of greasepaint.
After asking the girl next to me what to do, I wrote the basic
numbers, five and nine and so on, upon a piece of paper and
stuck it on the top of my box. Eyelashes were the trickiest job.
You had to heat the stuff for this in a spoon over a candle and
apply it sparingly with a match-stick, making blob upon blob
until the lashes were a fantastic length. If you once moved your
eyes the entire thing might smudge down on your face and you
had to start again. If you blinked too hard the blobs would fall
off.

Gilbert and Sullivan make-up had numerous variations. In
The Mikado, as a schoolgirl of Titipu, you had to be Japanese,
blotting out your own eyebrows and drawing others above them.
Mine were so black on the first night that I looked like a female
Boris Karloff. The stage manager, Harry Arnold, said mildly,
'Perhaps, Eileen, you ought to get someone to help you?' A
kind soul, meticulous and fussy, he was forever trying to keep
us quiet; he got so used to hissing 'Sssh!' that he even did it at
the stage furniture if this happened to scrape a little while it
was being moved.

I got my Mikado make-up right, but I admired myself most
as a lovesick maiden in Patience, very pale with prominent eyes;
really beautiful, I thought. Making up for the other operas, The
Gondoliers, The Pirates of Penzance, HMS Pinafore and the
rest, was fairly straightforward and I soon got the hang of it.
The dressing-room banter and its 'dirty jokes' did worry me at
first. Not that it was especially dreadful in the D'Oyly Carte.
One of the older girls had a way with bawdy stories, but half

the time I had no idea what she was talking about; I was petri-
fied lest the laugh might be against me. Here in the event my
steady convent training helped. Keeping a watch on the mirrors,
I laughed when the other girls did – probably a trifle too loud
and too long. Such simplicity as this soon vanished; before the
tour was over I understood all those dressing-room jokes, and
more.

It was important to get letters, otherwise you felt oddly cut
off; your friends, who had the list of touring dates, would write
direct to the theatre, and I heard quite often from Esme, Stella
and Helen, and all the time from my mother to whom I wrote
regularly and sent money. As a rule in those days, when you
walked down to the stage door in the late morning to collect
your mail, you would find the company assembled. That
autumn and winter more than seventy of us were touring.
Geoffrey Toye was our handsome conductor, and all the girls
were crazy about him. Henry Lytton, specialist in the harmless
flirtation, led the cast; Bertha Lewis, a formidable contralto, kept
an eye on him (she rather scared me); and we had, too, such
notable Gilbert and Sullivan names as Darrell Fancourt, Sydney
Granville, Charles Goulding, Elsie Griffin (the coloratura), Wini-
fred Lawson (soprano), Eileen Sharp (soubrette), and the charm-
ingly susceptible Leo Sheffield. Halfway through the tour he
fell in love with a much younger girl (whom he later married)
and gave up looking at anybody else. I had a real boy-and-girl
love affair with his good-looking son (younger than I was) whom
he adored: all very immature, much holding of hands, and the
occasional kiss.

III

From that fortnight at Wolverhampton we went to Newcastle
and on to Edinburgh. There I had my first flowers and notes sent
round from the front of the house (something that impressed
the other girls) and also an invitation to supper, which I accep-

ted. Again it proved to be a far older man, fifty no doubt, a
father-type like Esme but without Esme's gaiety. A widower
living with his sisters, he had influence in the city, knew someone on the Castle staff and took several of us up to the Rock.
Clearly he enjoyed motoring me around and entertaining me to
supper; if I felt a trifle bored I would ask one or two of the
others.

We stayed two weeks in Edinburgh, then three in Glasgow
(with a lot of rehearsal thrown in). I liked the big shops in
Sauchiehall Street but I was also haunted by the gloom of the
tenements. It seemed I was spying into poverty – maybe I was
sensitive here – to walk through the Gorbals on the south bank
of the Clyde and see these people sitting out on their doorsteps.
They learnt very early to be tough. A big restaurant near the
theatre would cram its dustbins with left-over food, half-loaves
of bread, oddments of every sort; and I watched what I had
never known in London, youngsters with bags clustering round
the bins to collect the food. Our landlady, who had a religious
bias, hung her room with texts, 'The Lord is my shepherd, I shall
not want,' which struck me as ironic, and 'God give me
strength', which in the circumstances was funny. Before going
out to explore the city, we turned the texts to the wall.

Such traditional theatre digs as we had then have disappeared.
Sometimes, if shabbier, more rough-and-ready, they reminded
me – with a vital difference – of the rooms I had known in
Fulham and Hammersmith. But on tour you had always to be
friendly with your landlady; no keeping haughtily apart.

It would be the day's talking point when the list of digs for
the next town was posted on the board. The whole company
joined in. Which were the best? Which landladies were clean-
est? Those best digs were intensely hard to book, for so many
players at that period were provincial favourites who did nothing
but tour and bespoke the same rooms from one year to the next.
But rates in general were reasonable, especially when two or
three were sharing. The landlady would greet you as Dearie or
Duckie; when she promised to look after you, she meant it. You

might be unfortunate, of course, as I was in Dundee, our next two weeks' date after Glasgow. The place was go-as-you-please and far from clean; the landlady, a 'fluff-under-the-bed' person, looked greasy and untidy. Late for dinner and glancing into the kitchen, I was sickened to see a pair of guinea-pigs scampering over the dresser, the table, and the food. After this I was unable to eat. The woman had a craze for pets: cats darting through the house, rabbits in hutches outside. Probably she had children, but we missed them. I merely recall the animals and the squalor. She may have had the obligatory heart of gold – we were not there long enough to find out.

A day's routine in the right digs would begin with a substantial late breakfast: bacon, egg, sausage, the lot. If you were in, you had high tea before the theatre – a pro.'s main meal is after the show at night. Two or three times a week the landlady would cook supper. On other evenings you might bring home fish-and-chips or whatever the local speciality was, black puddings or tripe; the table would be laid, and the landlady would make a huge pot of tea. Usually these rooms had a piano; many landladies had been on the halls, and on our last night in town we would get together for a sing-song, Ma joining us, as one pro. to another, with a sense of comradeship and a flurry of all the theatre's affectionate terms. These may not have meant much, but I liked them.

One creepy experience on the D'Oyly Carte tour I recall quite clearly. When we reached a town late on a night of wind and rain, two of our girls, who had not troubled to book in advance, called at the first address they were given. Next morning, when we were talking at the theatre, they came in thoroughly shaken. It seemed that the landlady had begun by refusing them. In the event she left them to drink tea while she put a room straight. Around dawn, peeping under the bed, the girls saw a large box pushed far back. It was a coffin. That was bad enough, but foolishly they lifted the lid, saw a corpse, and rushed down to the landlady in terror. Tearfully she said she had admitted them because they were in such trouble; anyway,

the coffin was to go out that morning. It went, and she was so
sad about it all that the girls stayed on – in another room.

IV

On Christmas Eve we arrived for five weeks in Liverpool, our
last date. It was the only Christmas – and this one was ideally
fine – that had meant anything to me; mostly I had hated them.
Helen Seldon came up, we visited friends of hers at a wild and
lovely place near Hoylake, and I got to my city digs in time for
the big theatre occasion, Boxing Night. The D'Oyly Carte gave
us a Christmas bonus of five pounds each, in those days a valuable present.

Just then my mother appeared to be living peacefully at
Brighton. Again in part-time work, nurse-companion to a young
woman, she was on the easiest terms with the family in a
pleasant, conventional house. I think the girl gave her the
affection I had failed to give, and she responded to it. Her ideas,
so old-fashioned to me, would have suited this family; she had
a quick sense of humour if people appreciated her, and she
always cared for her looks. At the time she was probably quite
proud of me and glad that I was in so famous a company as the
D'Oyly Carte.

Glad as I had been myself, I did need a change. I missed
London and was tired of touring from one room to another and
living in a trunk. It would be hard, I knew, to move up from
the chorus. Even if I could understudy, it might be years before
a part turned up in such a settled cast. I was unlucky to be a
mezzo. The showiest parts in Gilbert and Sullivan were for
sopranos, and two actresses were in line for the soubrettes I
might have managed. Recognising this, I asked Rupert D'Oyly
Carte if he would let me off my contract when the tour ended.
He was tolerant. Surely, he suggested, it might be foolish to
leave a long and regular engagement; my understudy chances
were genuine; I had been with them only a few months. His

patient arguments failed to persuade me. I had already made up my mind, and late in January, after our last night in Liverpool, I returned without regret to London and Stella and to another search for work.

CHAPTER FIVE

Chorus Girl

It felt grand to be back, living with Stella now in a large Chelsea studio; having the renewed freedom of the West End; riding on the bus-tops along Knightsbridge and past Hyde Park Corner towards Piccadilly and Marble Arch. That was relaxing enough, but I had to get work. Copying their addresses from *The Stage* newspaper, I began to toil round the agents' offices. They were scattered in Charing Cross Road and Shaftesbury Avenue: dismal places, all alike, rows of chairs, show-posters on the wall, and behind a glass partition the girl who asked for your details (mine were pretty thin). She was quite impersonal. You had to wait your turn, and, to begin with, you looked over the people with you, not in any friendly way but judging and estimating. Would they stand any better chance than you would? After a bit the ice would crack and you chatted politely until the girl called your name and you went into the inner room. Sometimes the agent scarcely glanced up; he simply confirmed the facts on your card, and that was all. But more often he would look at you, show a sudden interest, drop formal questions, and put on his come-hither tone: 'Now, dearie, tell me about yourself.' Some would ask to see your legs, important to a chorus-girl at any period; then you would be told to get on to such-and-such a theatre or to go to an audition that might suit you. At a London agent's, so different from those in New York, I never had a really awkward moment, just the pat or kiss, such a comment as 'You've got nice legs, duckie,' and the customary pinch on the bottom as you were leaving.

During the autumn of 1924 I auditioned for a musical comedy, *The First Kiss*, a hazy affair in a Spanish setting. I remember little about it. Auditions could frighten me. For the chorus you sang a number that you handed to the pianist as you came on. For a dancing show you did a small routine dance to the chorus of your chosen song; otherwise you just sang and were told to walk across the stage several times. In *The First Kiss* we merely drifted here and there as girls in a harem, making presumably graceful gestures – there were no set dancing numbers. We wore large head-dresses and yards of chiffon, with bits of elastic round our little fingers to give the floating garments an even greater float. The production, on one of the thinner shoe-strings, had nothing like the wardrobes I was used to later; in fact our costumes seemed to be dropping to pieces every night. When we opened at the New Oxford Theatre, which was rebuilt afterwards as a Corner House at the junction of Tottenham Court Road and Oxford Street, the notices were poor: James Agate, the drama critic, who came in late, thought 'the Spanish juice might have given out early'. Our leading lady, Désirée Ellinger, was a little person with a lovely voice; when I next saw her she was married to Geoffrey Carte, the throat specialist who had removed my tonsils. Courtice Pounds, the tenor, was a nice flirtatious man whose daughter Mary I would work with in *Bitter Sweet*. Mona Warren, in the chorus, became my life-long friend. A very able company; but we had to close after six weeks.

II

I had kept up my singing lessons, though not so seriously; by now I had admitted to myself that with neither the stamina nor the resolve – nor, most likely, the voice – I could never be a great opera star. It had to be musical comedy. Lots of girls I knew took dancing lessons, and I went to Carlotta Mosetti's studio (she was a teacher who had trained the actress June). It was by no means easy going; I was not limbered up, and after those first days at the *barre*, I woke in the morning so stiff that I could hardly hobble to a bath. Carlotta would telephone me commandingly: 'Take a good hot bath and work hard after it.' If you replied that you were suffering too much, she would merely say, 'Nonsense! If you don't keep going today, it will be worse tomorrow.' Obediently you went on torturing yourself, and she was right: the stiffness did vanish. A large, striking Italian, Carlotta had been a good dancer; she was an excellent coach with severe standards, plenty of patience, and a way of making you feel confident – she worked out an audition dance for me. Many of her pupils came to her when young and stayed for years; in a class with small teenagers I had to think of myself as an old retainer clopping behind.

I was not very secure in those days. Though it was easy to go to singing and dancing lessons full of myself, the moment I blundered in anything I would feel foolish, all assurance dropping. I was again the gauche schoolgirl who had to stand on the side-lines without skates or tennis racquet. Carlotta was clever at getting one over this. She had to be, for I knew only too surely how undecided I could be when dressing for a party or a date or an audition. I would put on a dress and take it off, put on another and take it off, try a blouse and skirt, try one necklace, then a second. Luckily there were not dozens to choose from; as it was, the room would look as if a burglar had been through it, and most probably I would go back in the end to the first dress of all and tear away to my appointment. It was a mixture of underrating myself and worrying far too much about my appearance. I could seldom agree that I looked really good.

Girls had to dress carefully according to their types. Thus some of them would wear showy, frilly clothes with ornate jewellery; others, tailored suits or – in vogue at the time – a tailored coat-frock. I decided on a pleated skirt, extremely well-made, and a polo-neck sweater. In the winter I wore tailored clothes, sports-style; in the summer for country week-ends, wide Oxford 'bags' which I pressed under the mattress – with these immensely wide trousers you had to be certain of a small waist. In the evening we had flowing short frocks, very feminine with layers on layers of chiffon. It was fashionable to wear a lamé pleated skirt just above the knee, a lamé jumper, and invariably a long string of beads which were knotted and allowed to flop down. (This is how Jackie, the flapper, looked in Coward's *Hay Fever*). Usually, satin shoes were dyed to match the dress. Hair, important to me, I wore bobbed or shingled with a kind of curl on the cheek.

Underwear just then could be a joy. When I was acting at Drury Lane in 1925 we could buy the most tempting lacy things in Soho, not very far from the theatre; and a Jewish woman sold us exquisite silk or pleated cami-knickers trimmed with lace. Sometimes she would tour the dressing-rooms; round her neck there dangled a long chain made of solid gold wedding-rings which was probably her notion of a bank account. I doubt whether we shall ever see such needlework as this again.

III

Someone had invited Stella to look after an enormous studio, in a block with others; a place that excited her because it had a north light. For me it was North Pole everything, deadly cold, so cold that I cut a hole in a blanket, put the blanket over my head, tied it at my waist with string, and always wore it in-doors. The studio was heated (so rumour had it) by a fire in the middle, with a chimney through the ceiling: we kept the thing going with coke, but it was never warm unless you were on top of it, and we had to pull our beds as close to it as we could. Off the studio, a vast place, were an icy little kitchen and a bathroom. I would leave the kitchen oven with its door open and dash to dry myself by it when I got out of the bath; Stella, much the hardier of us, was terrified that I would set the studio on fire. Esme Berkeley, when he called for me, talked of it as the barrack-room.

c

We were living here at the time of *The First Kiss*. When that
failed, the New Oxford management put on a Christmas panto-
mime, *Dick Whittington*, and some of us who had nothing to
do, auditioned for it – not too much of a strain because it was
a show that needed a large chorus split into three: small dancing girls, the Tiller Girls, and the medium-sized group, my
group, who both danced and sang. It was the expected panto-
medley: at least ten or twelve costume changes, some of them
very rapid ones at the side of the stage. At one minute, for the
song 'There are no flies on Auntie', you wore a zipped-on cat
suit and a cat mask; next, dashing off – and tossing off everything at the same time – you struggled into a costume with a
wide skirt and a hat like a daisy, and danced on again. Amusing, and exhausting as well: two performances on most days.
As pantomimes did, it ran for six weeks or so; Wilkie Bard was
our Dame, and Fred Whittaker the Cat. When it was over I
spent a lot of time with Mona Warren, hunting for another job.
Early in the spring of 1925 we got into *Love's Prisoner* at the
Adelphi, a musical play of the Napoleonic period set in a Cornwall as stagey as the names of its characters (people called most
improbably Black George Tregonning and Abel Polperro). The
star was Harry Welchman, who had a big public. He liked to
do a Douglas Fairbanks act, climbing over the wall and making
his entrance by leaping from a height into the centre of the
stage.

About now I met at Helen's a handsome naval sub-lieutenant,
Bill Sears. I had heard her speaking of him: his father, a
Protestant canon, lived in Gloucestershire near her guardian, and
she and Bill had known each other as girl and boy. One evening,
as I was leaving for the Adelphi, Bill joined me and arranged
to call after Saturday's show. We went to a club in Long Acre,
Chez Henri, to which other naval officers belonged and where
at that time you could see the young Douglas Byng and a
variety of other talent. When Bill had more money we might
go to the smarter Café de Paris. Helen and the rest believed that
he was in my life to stay; I thought myself that we might be

married, and I was happy to go about with a boy of my own age. Another young escort, Ben Hoare, of the banking family, took me to such places as the Gargoyle in Dean Street. I was with him also at a ghastly hunt ball. The hunting crowd had been only a name to me; though the women were distantly amiable and I got on with some of the older men, it was a pretentious party, formal and starched. I cannot say honestly that I was in love with Ben. In spite of his wealth he remained sensitive and shy, and his university had merely left him rather bitter. Obviously the two boys heard of each other. When I had a date with Bill I would get a brief telegram: 'Blast Bill.' It was not long before he, in his own turn, was wiring: 'Blast Ben.'

IV

Love's Prisoner had feeble notices. Soon Mona and I were searching frantically for a new show. Gossip was buzzing about a Broadway musical comedy entitled *Rose Marie*, a 'romance of the Canadian Rockies', with a score by Rudolf Friml and an exceptionally big chorus. An audition was fixed for Drury Lane; we practised feverishly, and on the morning joined a queue that stretched from the stage door right down the colonnade and round to the front of the house. I had never been to an audition so tense. They summoned us to the wings a group at a time. I was barely able to move. How I got to the centre of the stage, how my voice emerged, how I managed to dance, still puzzle me. (At that period, remember, we took nothing to steady the nerves, no tranquillisers.) Hurrying to escape as quickly as possible when my audition ended, I was utterly deaf to an American voice that shouted up from the stalls, 'Hey! Don't you want the job?'

Amused to see anyone so dazed – and well he might have been – the man told me to leave my name and address. I was in; so was Mona. At the Adelphi that night the news displeased

Harry Welchman. He asked the company to stay after the curtain, and when we had all met on stage he lectured us at length about leaving a sinking ship. Even at that hour he hoped he could keep the show afloat. I had no personal qualms about deserting the ship, floating or sinking; I was simply, and without reserve, delighted to have got into *Rose Marie*.

Rehearsals were stimulating, so professional and expert (though I recall how shocked we were one morning when someone ordered, 'Park your fannies, girls!'). Kathryn Scott, the chorus mistress and teacher of dancing, had crossed from New York, and most of the girls were highly trained, so it needed every scrap of concentration to match them. On the first day, when the chorus gathered, the whole sixty of us, the management kept asking for 'Reynolds'. Invariably two of us replied. Vain enough to think that I was the better, and wanting to avoid any muddle, I changed my name to Eileen Carey. Thereafter, whatever I did, I was 'Carey', and in my mind I am Carey still. It has had a curious psychological twist: it made me feel then that I had indeed broken away from my mother's influence, begun something completely new.

The famous *Rose Marie* number, 'Totem Tom Tom', depended less upon dancing than on discipline and precise timing. Everyone was in it, special dancers, showgirls, the whole crowd, dressed like totem-poles with identical tall hats, trouser-suits in bright satin with the totem-pole design, and soft slippers in the same colour. We entered singing, and, when the song ended, formed a great circle, each of us catching the next girl round the waist as in 'Oranges and Lemons', and sitting down with our legs stretched sideways. Instantly, in turn, each girl in the circle fell flat, one to the right, one to the left, until what seemed to be a huge coloured snake trailed across the stage; then, without breaking the rhythm, we got up and went the other way. The drill had to be exact; it was also tiring. Spare girls waited constantly in the wings to come on if anybody fell out, though few did. On the first night we were cheered so loudly that we had to appear again and again.

Sean O'Casey, who had not met me at that time, never forgot
what he described in *Rose and Crown* as 'the extraordinarily
beautiful slide and slip, shimmering with colour'. Most people,
too, admired the soft-shoe, high-kicking 'Pretty Things', for
which we wore chiffon elaborately pleated. *Rose Marie* tri-
umphed at once. From its first performance it was known to be
a winner, and I can recall now the carefree spirits in the dressing-room, the security that goes with a long run. Many of the
girls who were with me in the show married from it. Two of
them, Kathleen (a marvellously conscientious worker) and Lena
Fitchie, were mother and daughter, dancing side by side; Lena
could not have been more than sixteen or seventeen. In the end
Kathleen married Felix Edwardes, our producer or, as we should
say now, director.

Billy Merson was a friendly comedian and burlesque dancer.
Edith Day (Rose Marie La Flamme), our warm-hearted leading
lady, used to ask me to some of her parties, gay and extravagant
affairs at which one would meet most of the celebrities of the
time, including Edward Prince of Wales.

v

Helen was anxious to get me a flat of my own. Her trustees had
no objection, and before long I was installed in St Andrew's
Mansions, Dorset Street: not big – two small bedrooms and a
sitting-room – but convenient, likeable, and quiet. Helen furnished it for me so thoroughly that I used the same things after
my marriage and have some of them by me now. If I happened
to be late for the theatre there was always that reassuring taxi-
rank at the foot of Dorset Street; cabmen got to recognise you,
and if neither you nor the stage-door people had enough for the
fare, you could settle up at the end of the week. Stage girls get
this taxi complex. When Helen, as she often did, despatched
me to Drury Lane in her chauffeur-driven Daimler, the others
would rag me and call me 'Lady Carey'.

I was quite pleased with myself in those days. The stage job aside, I had begun to model hats and furs for leading photographers, well-paid work I slipped into by accident when a girl in the dressing-room who modelled for Dorothy Wilding was ill. She asked me to stand in for her if any dates came along, and to let her have the job back when she was better. I did this, but soon I had a modelling contract myself for such people as Dorothy Wilding and Janet Jevons. It was carefully mapped out. A cab took you to the shops – Bradleys it might be, or Marshalls, or small exclusive places – where you tried on the furs and hats; you were driven on with them to be photographed, and another cab returned the goods. Occasionally you could keep a hat or a blouse; never, alas, a fur coat. Once, when I was spending a week-end at Ben Hoare's country home, the *Tatler* carried a picture of me with the caption, 'Modelled by Eileen Carey'. It alarmed Ben's parents that their son should be seen about with a chorus-girl who modelled hats, but I don't remember feeling sinful. This was a week-end I quite enjoyed; for one reason or another I decided that I must go that Sunday to Mass, and the nearest place was a private chapel at the Gilbeys', a much warmer family with whom I could relax. With rich people of a certain type I used to feel deeply insecure.

It could not have been a busier life: modelling, dancing lessons and two matinées a week; and visits, when I could, to other shows – *No, No, Nanette*, *Hay Fever*, and so on – and to art galleries which I loved, though the dressing-room never saw why. Gallery-going was one thing I could do by myself. Otherwise, having been brought up at school in a group, I would be miserable if left for too long on my own (not that I wanted anyone in my flat at night after being with people all day and in the evening).

I could not analyse myself seriously, or ponder on the future. I had found so much that I had wanted. After years being ashamed of those drab rooms and the tales I drummed up for my schoolfriends, it meant much to have a real home. I could help my mother to better lodgings, though she remained inevitably pessimistic. For a few weeks she returned to live with me in Dorset Street, but I could not bear her interference with what she insisted on calling my 'unnatural life', and after yet another quarrel she preferred to leave me again for Brighton.

Bill was sent off to sea. We exchanged long, long letters; and for the time Ben took over. It was at this stage that Lee Ephraim, the American manager of *Rose Marie*, started asking me out to lunch and to supper-dances. A married man in his early forties, unassertive, kind, and husky-voiced, he attracted me more strongly than anybody I had yet known. Bill I accepted placidly: he was my boy. With Lee I felt an overwhelming emotion. For the first time, my instinct warned me to keep this secret; my religion must have been there in the background, though I had almost ceased to attend Sunday Mass, even the short service at twelve o'clock. Conscience was beginning to disturb me.

The first six months of *Rose Marie* flashed by. Helen, who was now engaged to be married shortly to Yule Elliott, suddenly planned to visit her friends in New York: would I care to go with her for the trip? I longed for the chance; but until Lee eased my mind, I felt dubious about losing the job at Drury Lane. He thought he might get me into the American cast of *Rose Marie* at the Imperial Theatre on Broadway; whatever happened, he would be crossing to New York himself. That resolved it. I said goodbye to the company, let the flat, and arranged a weekly payment to my mother. In the early autumn of 1925, profoundly excited, I boarded the *Mauretania* at Southampton.

CHAPTER SIX

New York

THE voyage was all I had hoped for. We sat at the Captain's table with Joseph Duveen, the art connoisseur, and the Norwegian explorer, Roald Amundsen. I joined in anything that was going on, and even sang at the ship's concert in the same programme as John McCormack, the tenor, who was crossing for recitals in New York. On landing we stayed at a big hotel close to the elevated railway along which trains clattered every few minutes. My first impressions were of terrific noise and a blaze of Broadway lights that affected me like the march-past of a stirring band – the same sensations, a lump in my throat and a tingling at the roots of my hair. Everywhere lights glittered into the sky; in my exhilaration I would have liked to stay up all night.

Next morning a woman's magazine rang up unexpectedly. I suppose they picked my name from the liner's passenger list, thinking I was a young actress keen to make good on Broadway. Soon a girl reporter hurried up for an interview and to take pictures of me in the enchanting clothes I ought to have had but did not. She was so flustered about her story that we tried to help by sifting through our wardrobes, Helen's and mine. Helen was much taller and bigger, but I had head-and-shoulder shots taken in her fur-collared coats hugged round my neck; and for other pictures I wore (I hope with dignity) evening dresses that were pinned in at the back. The best things in my own wardrobe were a frilly nightdress and a dressing-gown to match. It was a brisk morning, but since we saw neither story nor pictures, we could only hope the poor girl had got through.

In a day or two we moved to a smaller hotel, the Berkeley on 74th Street, where I stayed nearly all the time I was in New York. My primary task was to search for work. In Broadway the musical-comedy theatres were run mostly by the Shuberts; I resolved to hunt for a part myself and not to go straight to the *Rose Marie* chorus. Agents' offices, I learned, were much the same as in London, larger perhaps but as shabbily formidable; the men themselves were more determined. When I got an appointment with one of the top agencies for musical shows, the manager, who was himself interviewing, came round the desk, asked me a few questions, then instantly started to kiss and fondle me. I tried smiling hard and keeping the talk going, but it was useless: he merely got more amorous and seemed ready to make love there and then. Frightened, I became as shocked as a convent girl, as responsive as an iceberg. He struggled. I struggled. Finally he pulled himself together with some shred of dignity, saying that it was all my fault for getting him into such a state and he did not think I would be suitable for the small parts. I got away with relief. But when at the hotel that evening I had flowers from him and an invitation to dinner, I refused it: foolishly, I would realise, because the very next day I saw the result. Another agent had recommended me to a Broadway theatre: they were auditioning for some sort of operetta similar to *Lilac Time* – only a minor part, a spit-and-a-cough as we used to say, but after my song they did ask me, with some others, to wait for the manager. Who should arrive then to give his decision but the man I had snubbed on the previous night? Without surprise I heard him say, 'Sorry, I really don't think Miss Carey is suitable.' Two years later I was introduced to him at the Savoy in London; I could see from his smile that he remembered.

Never mind that. After a chance meeting with George M. Cohan on an office stairs, I picked up a job as a maid and understudy in the tour of *American Born*. Cohan, versatile man of

the theatre, had written it and was playing the lead himself. It
had already had its brief Broadway run; I knew at once it was
bad, a 'vehicle' which even its author (who got away with most
parts) could not make into a true comedy. He had set it,
rashly, in England at somewhere called Malbridge Hall. He
acted the 'Master of Malbridge'; the leading lady (Joan Maclean),
whom I understudied, was described strangely as 'Lady Bertram, of the District,' and a domestic staff, as large as superfluous,
dsecended steeply through housekeeper, butler, second butler,
under-butler and groom, to my part, poor Annie, a maid.

With two or three weeks left before the tour began, I chased
about to find some modelling. The New York method was less
decorous than London's. In New York you entered a big studio
full of small, screen-divided sets for the several advertisements.
One would contain a sofa; another, kitchen equipment; a third,
a bed. Posing for negligées on a fur sofa was like being in a film.
They shouted rapid instructions: 'Arms a little higher . . . leg
a little lower . . . one knee over the other.' Once you had
finished, you went off for another get-up, possibly pyjamas. I
did a lot with stockings, all magazine work, and, for a different
client, nothing but chocolate-box lids and biscuit tins. For these
you were photographed grinning broadly, your head by itself
or perhaps with a fur round the chin. Or you would be taken
in a more or less summery dress, sniffing at a bunch of violets.
In a few weeks I earned quite a bit, but too soon I had to leave
to rehearse with Cohan.

One of the friends Helen had come to New York to see was
a girl who had been at school with her. Now a hospital nurse,
Babs Dodge introduced me to some college boys who were devoted to football, never at any time my favourite sport. One of
them did lend me a long racoon coat, fashionable then and
valuable when looking for work. I would meet him for coffee,
go to the matches, and generally lead him on, but on the very
eve of the tour he shattered me by saying that since we were
not to meet again, he would like to have his coat back. And he
had it.

II

Lee, who reached New York before the tour started, was sorry I had signed on with Cohan; I would have been happier with the girls in *Rose Marie*. Well, I knew it was an unwise move; had I been in *Rose Marie* he could have helped me. I was a raw beginner, brave enough to put on a front when job-hunting, but when at work quickly put off by a catty remark. I could not believe in either my looks or my talent. No matter; I was extremely glad that Lee was with me in New York. We understood each other perfectly; he took me to the theatres and important night-clubs, the New Amsterdam Roof on 42nd Street, the Cotton Club in Harlem. All of this made me feel much worse at having to leave him to go off on tour, asking why I had made such a blunder. I wonder today what stopped me from returning home with Helen and getting back my part at Drury Lane. People I met in New York were simply acquaintances; people I was most anxious to see were from England. So what was wrong? Or what prevented me from joining *Rose Marie* at the Imperial? Maybe I believed I was improving myself in this sketch of a part. That was ridiculous, but it must have been fate. If I had not gone with Cohan I would not have met Joan Maclean; and unconsciously she altered my life.

American Born duly went the rounds of Philadelphia, Washington, Baltimore, Detroit and Cleveland, Ohio. I hated it. I was not much of a hand at understudy rehearsals. Given a chance I might have risen to the challenge, but there was nothing in the principal part to bring the best out of me, and I was so gauche and unresponsive that the producer must have been climbing up the wall. He got no higher than I did.

Somewhere one evening they telephoned me in the agitation known only to stage managers. I must come to the theatre early: Miss Maclean was ill, 'Lady Bertram' was waiting. I knew her lines all right. Her ordinary morning and evening

dresses fitted me, though I was rather taller and bigger. The
trouble was a riding habit for the main scene; they had never
dreamt of getting a second habit, and the boots were killing.
Obviously I wouldn't be able to move in them – it took ages
to pull them off. There, with the habit bursting at the seams, I
had to have a few lines written in so that I could carry on the
wretched boots with an appropriate excuse. We were ready at
last; I had made up and was about to go down to the wings
when what happens to every understudy happened to me – her
Ladyship walked in, determined to play. The balloon burst. Back
I went to Annie in her black taffeta dress and demure white
apron.

George Cohan was a dapper little man, quick at repartee.
Liking me, he made the usual advances, but he was not in the
least unpleasant when he understood that I loved someone else
and was no good at sleeping around. Without him I would have
been drearier than ever, wholly lost. If possible he would go
with me to a movie in the afternoon; at night he improvised
supper parties in his hotel suite. While all this was going on,
Ben Hoare, a most conventional type of Englishman, was in
New York with relatives. When he came to see me, travelling
out to either Philadelphia or Washington, he asked to meet
Cohan after the play. In the dressing-room I heard George's
whisper, 'Surely, Eileen, this isn't the one you threw me over
for?' No, I said, it was not; but I did not add anything.

Lee was in New York again, looking after some of his own
shows, and for a part of the tour I could get down to him at a
week-end, even if it meant starting the journey on Sunday
night – we seldom had a Monday performance – and returning
early on Tuesday in case we had to rehearse. But I could not
help feeling trapped, sitting round day by day, week by week,
going on at night for Annie's three lines and feeling more and
more inferior. Those months on tour with the D'Oyly Carte
had been so much more rewarding: we had long rehearsals and
a lot to learn. Daisy Belmore, a dear old actress who was the
housekeeper in *American Born*, used to lecture me on wasting

my years and my looks. How sorry I would be, she said, not to have been kinder to Cohan; he would have helped my stage career. Theoretically, I admit, her advice was sound. It was not the advice for me.

III

The tour dragged to its end in Cleveland. Back in New York I re-booked at the Berkeley and went to a singing teacher. His opening lesson, scales and so forth, was fairly straightforward; he thought my voice worth-while. The second lesson was a shade more active, an embrace, then scales, then more embraces and more scales. A large, fierce man, he was not at all appealing. At the third lesson we began with scales, he chose a piece for me to study, and we stopped for coffee; here, he said paternally, he had better give me some advice. I was exceedingly naïve: many people in a city like New York would try to make love to me, and one day (he added hopefully) I might be getting back to him. It was time for me to explain sweetly that there was already someone I was fond of and – with what grace I could – to step out of both the lesson and the dangerous romance.

Dancing next. At Ned Waven's beehive of a school I was luckier. In room upon room they taught musical-comedy tap-dancing, advanced level and second level; I chose the course for first-year pupils, several hours a week, hard work and no non-sense. It was so impersonal that no one could be nervous. When George Cohan, who was waiting to put on a revue, suggested me for a small part, I hesitated. Another cross-roads: ought I to remain now where I had a few friends and could find work, or would it be wiser (as at heart I believed it might) to sail back to England? I had been worried by exaggerated telegrams from my mother to say how seriously ill she was; Lee had also been urging me to return. Not long before Christmas 1925 I had been at his Algonquin Hotel party for English players away

from home (Edna Best and Herbert Marshall were two of them);
I had several 'singing telegrams' from England, always comic
when a little page-boy hurried up to sing you the message. Bill,
who was still at sea, had sent me a present, and to get it I had to
go miles to the post-office and sign many forms. It was a handbag. Reading his letter, I felt wistful, longing for the simplicity
of a relationship I had thought of again and again.

The choice, to go or stay, was pressing. On a dismal cold
afternoon I was at the Berkeley, planning my life and re-
planning it, when Joan Maclean rushed in excitedly with a
script. She had been asked, apparently, to act in an Irish play
with a strange title. Knowing I was Irish, though educated in
England by nuns who taught a 'lady-like' accent, she imagined
I could help her with the Dublin brogue. The book she left with
me was *Juno and the Paycock*, a tragi-comedy set during the
'troubles' of the year 1922 in 'the living apartment of a two-
roomed tenancy in a tenement house in Dublin'. On the spot I
began to read the story of 'Captain' Boyle, the slow peacock-
strutting waster of the taproom; 'Juno', his wife; 'Joxer' Daly,
his hanger-on; the Boyles' pregnant daughter, and their tragic
son.

Though it had been immensely applauded in London, where
it was still running with its company of Irish Players from the
Abbey Theatre, I had not heard of it before, and in that New
York room I read it with astonishment: delight at the richness
of Sean O'Casey's humour mingled with awe at moments of
tragic emotion like nothing else I had known. Here was the
grave nonsense of the scene between the Paycock and Joxer in
the first act, one that, though I could not guess it then, would
be a classic of the stage. Here too – and this moved me particularly – was the scene between Mary Boyle and her lover Jerry
Devine who, though he knows of 'another man', does not yet
know that the girl is pregnant:

JERRY: Your mother has told me everything, Mary, and I
have come to you . . . I have come to tell you,

Mary, that my love for you is greater and deeper than ever . . .

MARY (*with a sob*): Oh, Jerry, Jerry, say no more; all that is over now; anything like that is impossible now!

JERRY: Impossible? Why do you talk like that, Mary?

MARY: After all that has happened.

JERRY: What does it matter what has happened? We are young enough to be able to forget all those things. (*He catches her hand.*) Mary, Mary, I am pleading for your love. With Labour, Mary, humanity is above everything; we are the Leaders in the fight for a new life. I want to forget Bentham, I want to forget that you left me – even for a while.

MARY: Oh, Jerry, Jerry, you haven't the bitter word of scorn for me after all.

JERRY (*passionately*): Scorn! I love you, love you, Mary!

MARY (*rising, and looking him in the eyes*): Even though . . .

JERRY: Even though you threw me over for another man; even though you gave me many a bitter word!

MARY: Yes, yes, I know; but you love me, even though . . . even though . . . I'm goin' . . . goin'. . . . (*He looks at her questioningly, and fear gathers in his eyes.*) Ah, I was thinkin' so . . . You don't know everything!

JERRY: (*poignantly*): Surely to God, Mary, you don't mean that . . . that . . . that . . .

MARY: Now you know all, Jerry; now you know all!

JERRY: My God, Mary, have you fallen as low as that?

MARY: Yes, Jerry, as you say, I have fallen as low as that.

JERRY: I didn't mean it that way, Mary . . . it came on me so sudden, that I didn't mind what I was sayin' . . . I never expected this – your mother never told me . . . I'm sorry . . . God knows, I'm sorry for you, Mary.

MARY: Let us say no more, Jerry; I don't blame you for thinkin' it's terrible . . . I suppose it is . . . Everybody'll think the same . . . it's only as I expected – your humanity is just as narrow as the humanity of the others.

JERRY: I'm sorry, all the same . . . I shouldn't have troubled
you . . . I wouldn't if I'd known . . . If I can do anything
for you . . . Mary . . . I will. (*He turns to go.*)

I read, too, Juno's great lament when, knowing her son was
dead, she found herself repeating what a bereaved mother had
cried earlier. Immediately after this the play ended with an
amazing scene of tragic irony, the entrance of the two drunken
men and the repetition of a phrase, a few words, that one day
would be in all the quotation books: 'I'm telling you . . .
Joxer . . . th' whole worl's . . . in a terr . . . ible state o' chassis!'
Deeply stirred, I knew beyond doubt that I must meet the
dramatist – Sean O'Casey.

IV

The reading had settled my mind already disturbed by my
mother's telegrams. I must get home to London and to the
theatre, to one theatre especially. The only person I consulted,
George M. Cohan, said, 'I think perhaps you would be wiser to
go back.'

So it was arranged; again the ship would be the *Mauretania*.
On my last night in New York Cohan took me to a party given
by Mayor Walker who had a gift for collecting young stage
people; in the small hours, and with the party still on, I returned
to the Berkeley, finished my packing, and drove down to the
wharf in the daybreak. Cohan and many others were there to
see me off, all flowers and gaiety. On board the Captain greeted
me as an old friend. Babs Dodge was in the ship. Though a
bout of sciatica marred the crossing, that was better when we
docked at Southampton, and Lee, whom I had cabled, met us.
With him we motored up to London, and I could not have been
happier that evening to be back in the peace of St Andrew's
Mansions. It was, I knew, my real home. Almost at once I asked
Lee about Sean O'Casey's play. 'Yes,' he said immediately, '*Juno
and the Paycock*. I'll take you to it, Eileen, tomorrow night.'

CHAPTER SEVEN

Acting in Sean's Plays

THAT night would mean much to both of us. I am a fatalist, an absolute fatalist. No matter what we plan, I believe we have very little control over our destinies. Lee was as unaware as I was of the effect *Juno* would have on our lives. The play had been running for some months, but the Fortune Theatre* was full and the night as powerful as I had known it would be. The truth of both writing and performance enthralled me: Arthur Sinclair and Sara Allgood; Sydney Morgan as Joxer ('A cup of tay's a darlin' thing, a daaarlin' thing'); Harry Hutchinson, Cathleen Drago, and Kathleen O'Regan; and Maire O'Neill as the garrulous Maisie Madigan who is described with such relish:

> She is ignorant, vulgar, and forward, but her heart is generous withal. For instance, she would help a neighbour's sick child; she would probably kill the child, but her intention would be to cure it; she would be more at home helping a drayman to lift a fallen horse.

I had to see Sean O'Casey. Lee I admired as a business man of the theatre; now I was determined to meet a creative artist. During supper at the Savoy I asked Lee if he could get me an introduction. Perhaps, if they sent *Juno* on tour, I could understudy the daughter Mary ('Mother, the best man for a woman is the man for whom she has the most love')? It might be the

* It had opened at the old Royalty in Soho on 16 November 1925 and gone later to the Fortune.

start of better work. I had had no experience except in the chorus, and in *American Born* which barely counted, but when you are young and ambitious (and I was both) the foolish side seldom occurs to you. *Juno* haunted me that night. All these years later I think it must have been the pregnant girl that appealed to me so greatly. I might well have been in the same position. I understood Mary Boyle, and I was by no means far enough from the convent not to think as she did.

I knew Lee would keep his word, for the play had startled him equally. An emotional man, Jewish, with no privileged up-bringing, he had felt the full impact. Soon now he telephoned. Yes, James Bernard Fagan, the manager of *Juno*, would see me in his office at the Fortune, opposite the stage door of Drury Lane, and Sean O'Casey himself would be there. Striving that afternoon to look my best, I was as nervous as I had always been at any interview or audition.

In the Fortune office Fagan and Sean were sitting at the desk together. As I entered, the first person to greet me, rising with both his hands outstretched, was Sean himself. 'You've nothing to worry about,' he said with a soothing understatement, and beckoned me to sit beside him. I ceased to be nervous; it was clear that he admired me, and that first gesture and the timbre of his voice put me at ease. His eyes were deeply set; he had such an expressive face that I never realised the weakness of his sight. He wore an orange muffler, a trench-coat with a belt fastened tightly round it, and heavy boots; the office must have been cold, for we all kept our coats on. I told Sean how *Juno* had thrilled me, and how much, if it toured, I would like to understudy Mary Boyle. Fagan was the man who should have been interviewing me, but I hardly noticed him until he said goodbye and in the usual formula asked for my address. All I wished was to stay there talking to Sean.

Within a few days Fagan rang up: could I go to see him at the Fortune (a theatre Sean called rudely a 'kip')? Again I dolled myself up for anything that might happen – but what could it be? Sean was in the office, his welcome even warmer.

Then Fagan spoke: Kathleen O'Regan, who was cast as Nora in Sean's next play, *The Plough and the Stars*, had been taken ill; rehearsals had begun, and the production must open in a fortnight.

Sean looked at me. 'I think,' he said, 'you could play this part very well.'

It was impossible, of course. I had done nothing in the straight theatre. How could I? While I was talking Sean quietly handed me the script and asked me to come back next day so that we could go through the lines. Fagan was not so swiftly bowled over. It was clear that before I got the part I would have to read to him; yet, just as clearly he was in a fix and had to have an actress.

That evening, half-dazed, I read *The Plough*, and found its blend of comedy and black tragedy even more moving than *Juno*. The period was the Easter Week rebellion of 1916. My character, Nora, pregnant wife of a Citizen Army Commandant, was distraught on hearing of his death. Earlier Sean had described her as 'a young woman of twenty-two, alert, swift, full of nervous energy, and a little anxious to get on in the world. The firm lines of her chin are considerably opposed by a soft amorous mouth and gentle eyes. When her firmness fails her, she persuades us with her feminine charm.'

As always the prospect of an audition scared me; I still had sciatica and had to be doped to blur the pain. Yet Sean was so bent on having me that I got through the part with him – and in front of Fagan – and they arranged for me to be coached, as Kathleen O'Regan had been, by the veteran actress Kate Rorke. Between my lessons and rehearsals at the theatre there was little time to worry. In rehearsal I had no sympathy at all from Sara (Sally) Allgood, who was Bessie, the street fruitseller, but Maire O'Neill, as the tenement neighbour, and Arthur Sinclair as the carpenter Fluther Good, did as much as possible to help. It was an incredible fortnight. Sean was infatuated and did not hide it. Fagan's wife, Mary Grey, was cruelly resolved to dislike me – God knows why, for she was an accomplished actress and I had

nothing whatever to work on. Unsure of myself, almost hypno-
tised into playing Nora, I had to press forward in a dream that
a single word of discouragement would break.

II

The night arrived. Thanks to Maire O'Neill, Sinclair, and Sean
himself, I did get through it. Many theatre people remembered
me with flowers and telegrams. Several were from the *Rose
Marie* company – Drury Lane girls were always running across
the road to know how I was – and I heard also from a London
manager, Archie de Bear, whom I had met with Lee and who
thought that I might audition for his revues. Before curtain-rise
Sean came in to talk for a few minutes, showing his own confi-
dence and helping mine. The night's atmosphere was inevitably
unsettled, for in and out of the theatre people were talking of
the General Strike which had disrupted the country and had
only just ended. But during the play the house was marvellous,
and so (when they appeared) were the notices. The Irish Players,
Herbert Farjeon wrote, 'again acquitted themselves beyond all
praise'. I must have fitted into the ensemble. At supper Lee had
said that for anyone so inexperienced I had done wonderfully
and would improve every night. Strange that he should have
been the consoler – already Sean was a trifle sullen about our
association.

For two or three weeks I did improve steadily. Sinclair, and
even Sally, agreed that no one had done Nora's mad scene better: 'I feel as if my life was tryin' to force its way out of my
body . . . I can hardly breathe . . . I'm frightened, I'm frightened.' Possibly I could understand the girl because long before,
when I was working at Burgess Hill, I had seen how the deranged could behave.

The dream ended sharply. Kathleen O'Regan, who was due
to return on a Monday, came in to the previous Saturday's
matinée and insisted on playing that night. Equally, I suppose,

I could have insisted that I was under contract until Monday: if this had been honoured I would have gone on understudying. My dresser, Mrs Earle, also looked after me at home; I could confide in her about anything. Now she said angrily, 'You really shouldn't do this. You have invited people to come in tonight, and you have improved so much. There is no reason why Miss O'Regan shouldn't wait.' No reason at all, but my temper was up. I was not thinking of the future, nor of being tactful, nor working for myself. I simply grabbed my belongings and left the theatre; and on Monday I telephoned that I would not return to understudy.

So this was it, back in the old groove. I had to get some work. I drifted into a familiar routine, going out to dine with my boy-friends. Sean often rang me up. He did not argue. Though he thought I might have been unwise to give up Nora, it was right to cut away from 'a nest of jealousies'. Had I any other plans? He asked me over to tea at his lodgings in Trafalgar Square, Chelsea – not a successful meal. The landlady, called appropriately Mrs Sparrow, was thin and small with a pinched face. She was also suspicious. Having brought the tea and left the door open – Sean shut it firmly – she found excuse upon excuse to come back. Every time Sean tried to kiss me, there was Mrs Sparrow at the door, asking fatuously if we were all right. We were not; this was ruining Sean's first attempt at courtship, and he said glumly, 'I think we'd be better off in the bloody Park.' So to Hyde Park we went; Sean's first kiss was a very small peck before we parted.

My need for him still puzzled me; we were so obviously different. But I understood what a compliment he was paying to see so much of me when the world was honouring him as a great dramatist. He talked to me as one intelligent person to another. Though I met Lee often, Sean's personality was conquering – I simply knew that someone irresistible had entered my life.

During the autumn of 1926 Lee cast me for the soubrette in
The Street Singer, a musical comedy with a frivolous book by
Frederick Lonsdale, which was going on a short suburban tour.
For twelve weeks, twice nightly, we played in an outer circle
of London theatres (only a few are left now), Croydon, Wimbledon, Lewisham, Stoke Newington, Chelsea Palace. My sciatica
was worse. Frequently Sean, who was bored by the piece but
anxious for my health, came to see me and to bring me home.
Just before we opened he had written: 'Remember the advice of
Saint Teresa: "Pray as if everything depended upon God; work
as if everything depended upon yourself." '

He was almost inseparable in those days from an eccentric
Bohemian character, Billy McElroy, a wealthy coal-merchant
and a friend of Augustus John and Oliver St John Gogarty.
Billy, who financed the transfers of *Juno* and *The Plough* from
Dublin, had recently made a lot of money from the sale of slag.
It lay in huge waste-heaps round the coal-mines that had closed
at the General Strike, and Billy saw that he could get rid of it
to anyone who needed some kind of fuel. Sean teasingly said
because of Billy life had slowed down and trains were going at
half-speed. Every night the pair of them would join Augustus
John at a Sloane Square restaurant popular with authors and
artists. They were a remarkable trio. Billy was tall and buoy-
antly genial, with a crown of fine white hair. Augustus, com-
manding and bearded, with large searching eyes, wore his hair
swept back and fairly long. Beside them was the lean figure of
Sean, also with uncommon eyes that, because of his indifferent
sight, seemed to be strained and deep-set. I met them often at
the Queen's, and it was lucky for me that Augustus approved.
Unless he was talking himself, he could be as intolerant in
company as Sean was. A man might wander up to our table
and begin bravely, 'Oh, Mr John (or Mr O'Casey), I'm so-and-so
and it's so good to meet you.' Utter silence – both Sean and

Augustus had this unnerving trick of treating an intruder as
if he were not there and as if none of it could be happening.
The stranger would murmur unhappily, 'Well ... er ... goodbye,' and Augustus and Sean would each give a slight, courteous
nod. That was over; one way of settling a difficulty. Sean admired Augustus. 'I've made a great buttie of him,' he wrote in
a letter to Ireland at this time, 'he's a splendid fellow. Says I'm
a great dramatist, slaps me on the back for breaking every
damned rule of the stage.'

I got to know Sloane Square well. Sir Barry Jackson, from
the Birmingham Repertory and then a London manager, had
leased the Court Theatre. In the spring of 1927 he engaged me
for a play by Eden Phillpotts, whose comedy, *The Farmer's
Wife*, had run for nearly three years. *The Blue Comet* could not
have been less like it. Set in Hampstead, it was about people
waiting for the end of the world. The world survived and the
play did not; but through its month's run I understudied the
leading lady, Cecily Byrne, besides having a short bit of my
own, shouting 'Piper! Evening piper!' as a newsboy offstage.
Understudy rehearsals did add to my experience – that was all.
On the night the *Comet* closed, *Rose Marie* ended its two years
at Drury Lane. Lee was eager for me to be there at the final
curtain; somehow I made it by taxi and sat with him in a stage
box, watching with tears in my eyes, thinking how much my
life had changed during the run of a single musical comedy. I
had met Lee, to whom I was so emotionally close that night; I
had been to America and back; and I had found Sean.

IV

Sean loved me to be with him and told me that he would like
us to marry. But he was nervous, a little perplexed. Our lives
were so different. Could we really settle together? Though he
came back to this repeatedly, I had no fear of the outcome:
gradually I saw less of Lee and less of Ben. When writing over-

seas to Bill I never told him of my dilemma. I was probably wrong. It was not dishonesty, just that my training had obliged me to act for myself, and unconsciously to play safe.

A solution was at hand. Lee told me of *The Desert Song*, a new American musical play that was booked for Drury Lane early in April 1927. He was certain that I was good enough to understudy Edith Day – again in the lead – and to take minor parts; and being far more confident now and singing quite well, I survived a tough audition with a number from the show. That was encouraging; but then at lunch Lee said bluntly that I must stop making a fool of him. Everyone knew by now that I was dividing my time between him and Sean O'Casey. If I took the *Desert Song* job, I should have to choose at once: it was only fair.

I went to Sean. Scorning musical comedy, he could not see that it would be very rash to reject an important understudy at Drury Lane. I must decide for myself: did I want to stay with him, or not? I was in an agonising position, and I am sure Lee never realised the acute feeling of guilt I would have if we remained together. Even if he had divorced his wife, at that stage of my Catholic beliefs I could not have thought it right to marry him. Moreover, I knew I could not give up meeting Sean: he had become essential. There was only one answer – I refused the offer from Drury Lane.

For a few weeks, nothing. But now Barry Jackson asked me to play Minnie Powell in Sean's earliest success, *The Shadow of a Gunman*, which he was presenting at the Court. I don't know whether this was Sean's idea; I rather believe it was. During the first weeks Synge's *Riders to the Sea*, in which I was cast among the 'keeners' at the island wake, was staged as a curtain-raiser. Recalling *The Plough*, it terrified me to go back to the Irish actors, and rehearsing for Minnie was a nightmare.

The part was that of an aspiring, and finally tragic, tenement girl of twenty-three, who tries to help a fellow lodger she believes to be a gunman in hiding. In Sean's words: 'The fact of being forced to earn her living, and to take care of herself, has given her an assurance beyond her years. She has lost the sense of fear (she does not know this) and, consequently, she is at ease in all places and before all persons, even of a superior education; so long as she meets them in the atmosphere that surrounds the members of her own class.' At rehearsal we worked to an only too familiar pattern. Sara Allgood was as horrid to me as Arthur Sinclair and Maire O'Neill were kind. Harry Hutchinson, then a young man, acted the supposed gunman, Donal. A sweet person but very shy, he could be awkward in a love scene: when he should have looked at me, he gazed to high heaven instead, and I was left stranded.

Notices were encouraging, and during the run, which lasted for two months, I grew into the part. In *Riders*, besides my share in the keening, I understudied Cathleen Drago as Nora. Margaret O'Farrell, Maire O'Neill's daughter, was another of the mourners. Kneeling downstage and wailing away, we would be peeping under our shawls to see whether we knew anyone in the house. Sally, in her full surge, would move over to us, turn slightly from the audience, whisper, 'Why don't you cover your faces up? They're not looking at *you*,' and slip back without break into her high tragic performance.

V

Yet again – it was like an everlasting serial – I had my mother to live with me at St Andrew's Mansions. She was pleased to come, even if I was certain it could not work: nothing did whenever I went back on a decision I had thought about carefully. She could not have chosen a worse time – I had never been so preoccupied. The flat was not in her favourite part of London. Acting in the *Gunman*, or racing here and there, I was seldom at home and she began to pry into my things, even reading my letters before I had them: an infuriating liberty. A letter belongs to the person it is written to, and I would never open other people's, and after the convent I was naturally possessive. Furious both when she read my correspondence and forced my desk, I flamed out at her. Aggrieved, she said she was merely trying to help me lead 'a good life'.

I presume she was lonely. Most nights I would go on somewhere from the theatre and lie late in bed next morning: a crime (no less) that had angered her in *Rose Marie* days. Back to the old nagging, the 'unhealthy life', the disgraceful sight of a young person in bed at half-past ten or eleven o'clock. Now and then I had Sean home for a light lunch. He and she never got on; if it were midday they might not meet, but they would have to when he brought me in at nights and she was there shouting about my lateness. Being lonely she was drinking once more, and it was a weakness he could not forgive; I would offer him a cup of tea while she fussed on behind me, saying pointedly that it was a shocking hour for any man to have a girl out with him.

I noticed that if Ben were the man, she never argued. He just saw me to the door and she never met him; but she went on repeating that it would be far better if I married a rich young fellow than muddled myself up with this Irish playwright. The theatre meant absolutely nothing to her; it never had. She had been to *Juno*, presumably to the *Plough* and the *Gunman* – I am sure she must have seen me at the Court – but she objected to the stage as a career and ignored any connection with it. If this sounds unimportant, it was vital to me. So much was on my mind, and how could we discuss any of it? To make conversation I would have to invent a lot of things that might please her – and what was that but returning to the fantasy-world of the convent? It was absurd to try to live together: I asked her whether she would like to go, and without argument she went. After only a month in Dorset Street she was happy to escape to Brighton.

VI

On most evenings during the *Gunman* Sean called at my dressing room. Practically every day we lunched together and walked
in Hyde Park while he told me about his new play, *The Silver
Tassie,* and his hopes for the second act. 'To hell with so-called
realism!' he wrote once, 'for it leads nowhere.' One realistic
distraction was my wire-haired terrier Bobby. Full of character
and totally untrained, he adored me. I found him alarming; if
we let him off his lead in Hyde Park or Kew Gardens, it would
be hours before we got him back. Glancing up at me, he would
dart off again, with Sean far behind, laughing uncontrollably.

I went on going to supper, or dancing, with the others. Lee
used to keep away from the Court, which was Sean's special
ground, but Ben would appear in evening dress and wait until
I had changed. Infallibly, late that night, the telephone would
be ringing: 'So you're home at last? Really, Eileen, you can't
think of marrying that man, he's not worthy of you.' Actually
Sean liked him, but there had to be limits. I remember a trivial
matter from those days. Ben invited me to the family coach at
Lord's for the Eton and Harrow match. Early that morning rain
was probable, disastrous to my fashionable dress and large hat.
Helen was on the telephone. 'If it does rain,' I groaned, 'I've
nothing to wear.' Don't worry, said this rich girl who practically
lived in her chauffeur-driven Daimler, she would go past Lord's
on a bus-top to see what other people were doing. Half an hour
later she rang back: they were in their regalia, it had begun to
sprinkle, and umbrellas were up. I risked all, put everything on,
between us we found an elegant umbrella, and I had a lovely
day. There was cricket too, but that was secondary.

Parting from Lee was most difficult. The only way to do it
was to go out with him and to tell him honestly. By bad luck
Sean happened to be at the flat when he called. I blurted out
my decision, and Lee looked at me in helpless despair. Without
saying a word he left the building: a wretched moment, for in

a sense I loved him still. 'How happy could I be with either . . .'
Sean, distressed for me as well as hurt, saw that it would be
better to leave me alone. Presently Lee rang up to say that I had
put him in an impossible situation – as, unwittingly, I had. We
talked on in tears, but I would not go back; it was my fate, and
I had decided. Loving both men in ways entirely different, I
was selfishly sorry for myself and not for Lee. My choice was
made; once accepted, it was an immense relief to know where I
stood, and that at last I could enter without misgiving into life
with Sean O'Casey.

CHAPTER EIGHT

Marriage

I COULD have predicted what my mother would do when she heard. Calling on Sean and using the clumsiest tactics, she told him, in effect, that he was going to destroy a young girl's life. Not really a step towards peacemaking. The worldly-wise might say that having had me educated as a 'lady' at a good convent, she would want my husband to be a man of position or, at least, security. A dramatist would be perilously insecure – that was true enough – and Sean was a Protestant, considerably older than I was and from a poor family. But marriage has to be a risk on both sides. If my mother objected to Sean, he objected as firmly to her: he thought she was insincere. But she was right in her fashion. We had not even contemplated our future. Once she had whisked off to Brighton, we were by ourselves and continually seeing each other. Billy McElroy disapproved; more than a little jealous, he believed Sean would be foolish to marry me, and I knew why: I was robbing him of a matchless companion. Now, whenever he met Sean, I was there as a third party, and hours they had spent together must be spent with me.

Usually I travelled by Tube from Baker Street to meet Sean at Sloane Square. On fine days we met halfway across the Park; he lived down at the Kensington Gardens end, and I was on the other side, right up near Marble Arch. I took great care with my appearance. Always noticing dress and colour, he would invariably tell me about them; he liked good legs, and skirts then were short and free. He was still absorbed in his play, now formally entitled *The Silver Tassie* after Burns's song, 'Go fetch to me a pint o' wine,' which he had heard Billy McElroy singing in the London coal office. Lennox Robinson had been to see him, declaring to Sean's pleasure that the play must go to the Abbey in Dublin.

He had left his Chelsea digs for an unfurnished flat in Clareville Street, tree-fringed, pleasantly old-fashioned, and just off Gloucester Road. They had sent across his desk and chair from Dublin, the sofa a carpenter-friend had made, his books, and a print of Giorgione's Sleeping Venus, mentioned in *The Plough and the Stars*. 'Oh, that's a shockin' picture,' says Fluther. 'It's nearly a derogatory thing to be in the room where it is.' With Billy at his elbow, Sean had found various divans, secondhand carpets, and glass-fronted bookcases of the type one might see in an office. More personally, he added some excellent pieces of china from the antique shops in King's Road. It was a sad accident when his friend, the actor Barry Fitzgerald, broke a prized Chinese vase, tall and glowing, that was kept on the floor. At my home in Ireland I still have Sean's chair and desk, his sofa, and most of the china. He had an instinct for the right thing. With his flair for sketching he could have been an artist if his eyes had let him.

I never wondered how the marriage would affect me. Sean's presence and his admiration were enough ('Eileen', he wrote to me, 'is my delight on the hills of vision, and the touch of her white hand is strength in the shadows of thought.') I had not considered a new part. In the evening we might dine out or go to a play; we were fully carried away by Robert Loraine's performance in Strindberg's *The Father* which he acted at the Savoy with a little piece by Barrie as a curtain-raiser. Next day Sean wrote a letter to Loraine which we both signed:

ROBERT LORAINE – A friend and I saw you last night, and saw you not; you were a great artist in a great play.

Strindberg, Strindberg, Strindberg – the greatest of them all. Barrie mumbling as he silvers his little model stars and

gilds his little model suns, while Strindberg shakes flame
from the living planets and the fixed stars.

Ibsen can sit serenely in his Doll's House, while Strindberg
is battling with his heaven and hell . . .

Kyrie Eleison, Robert Loraine, Christe Eleison.

EILEEN CAREY, SEAN O'CASEY

At other times Sean worked on the *Tassie* while I sat quietly
by. I had never felt more secure, troubled though I was by the
amount I owed for my dresses. Thanks to Lee, it had been simple
to run up the bills. Probably because I had such a vivid memory
of depending on cast-offs, I had been too extravagant. While
scraping through on richer people's help, I had lived too long on
my personality, my one real asset; then during *Rose Marie* and
after, I accustomed myself to buying the proper clothes I
needed. Because I had gone on for a while after the break with
Lee, the shops had sent in bill upon bill. It was not a matter I
could go to Lee about, so I had to confess to Sean, and without
a word he bore the entire responsibility.

II

Our marriage had to be planned. I wanted it to be in a Catholic
church. Sean, an agnostic, was one of the most truly moral men
I had known; if we had merely decided to set up house together,
this would have seemed sacred to him, but he was anxious to
do what I wished, and we undertook the intricate business of a
mixed marriage between Catholic and Protestant. Remarkably,
in Sean's own Chelsea parish we came upon a priest of advanced
views, Father Howell, who had memories of me as a schoolgirl.
Nothing at all disturbed Sean. He had been accustomed to
priests since his Dublin boyhood when his neighbours were
Catholics and he had learned their ways.

We had also to think about children. I loved them, and if
we had none I feared our marriage might fail (this in spite of

my panic a month or so later). Sean, again, did not fuss: he accepted equably the mixed-marriage obligation to bring up the children as Catholics. At the time I had no other desire.

The wedding was fixed for 23 September 1927 at the Church of the Most Holy Redeemer in Chelsea. It never occurred to me to wear white. Helen, who was now Mrs Yule Elliott (I had been a bridesmaid at their St Margaret's, Westminster, wedding in 1926) lived in Charles Street, Berkeley Square; I stayed in the house for a few days with my dresser, Mrs Earle, and Helen gave me an expensive blue chiffon dress and a blue coat in a woollen material with a grey fur collar. Captain Corby promised to give me away; Sean chose Billy McElroy as his best man. By then I was pregnant. On the morning of the twenty-third I felt very sick, but Mrs Earle, my mother-figure at the time, looked after me gently. I would not have dreamt of telling my own mother about the child which had only just started.

I had arranged to drive to the church alone with Captain Corby. At the twelfth hour we had a companion, my terrier Bobby, who had been shaved and decorated with a large bow, and who seemed so miserably unlike himself that he went with us and waited in the car until all was over. Arriving too soon, we had to be driven round and round the Park. Sean, just free of a trying bronchial attack, was late but exceedingly spruce in what he called his best plum-coloured suit. With cine-cameras buzzing away on pictures for the evening newsreels, the church was uncommonly noisy. Only my intimate friends were there, and though I was alarmed when, before the service began, my mother, highly agitated and in the most sombre garments from head to foot, attempted to speak privately to Father Howell, she did return to her seat and endure it all without protest.

As in every farce the ring was mislaid, and minutes passed like hours until Billy discovered it. A civil wedding in the presbytery followed the ceremony at the altar; when at length we walked down the nave I was a little dazed. Sean, my hand firmly in his, was more matter-of-fact; noticing the set of his mouth, I knew he was much the stronger. For a second, right at the

back of the church, I saw Lee, and it would be false not to say
that I wanted to rush over and explain why this had had to be.
Sean had seen nothing; and at the moment he was holding my
hand even more tightly.

Helen had ordered our wedding breakfast at Charles Street.
In sudden dismay I calculated that we would be thirteen at
table. Not that Sean, stoical about the whole business, would
have cared whether there were thirteen or thirty, but to my
superstitious mind thirteen would not do; nothing would satisfy
me until after frantic telephoning a friend of Helen's called Pat
promised to be the fourteenth guest. We were a mixed crowd,
Billy McElroy, Captain Corby, my stage friend Mona (married
to the writer, singer, and pianist, B. C. Hilliam or 'Flotsam'),
and Alison Gaunt (Duncan) from Nutford House. My mother
was thoroughly amiable and found that she and Billy McElroy's
wife could console each other. Sean, who enjoyed talking to
Corby, stuck it out as late as half-past four, when he had to
return to Clareville Street for his luggage and I had to change
for our honeymoon journey to Dublin.

III

In the boat from Holyhead we were joined by one of Billy's
sons, Willie McElroy, crossing for a throat operation by the
author Oliver St John Gogarty, then Dublin's best ear-and-
throat surgeon. Proving that, on the Irish Sea at least, he was a
first-class sailor, Sean roamed round the deck with Willie while
I stayed in my cabin. At Dun Laoghaire Gogarty himself was
waiting on the quay on one of the gloomiest of mornings, cold
under a heavy sky. Having had Ireland praised to me since
childhood as the one real Utopia, I was practically in tears with
disappointment. Sean humoured me. We were bundled (the
only word I can think of) into Gogarty's sports car, and, before
we could think, off it whizzed like a rifle bullet. Thrown backwards, we sat down with a thud, squashing the flimsy fibre

suitcase Sean used for his overnight things. Though we were bound for Howth, nine miles to the north of Dublin, it appeared to be quite a short drive; and when we drew up at the hotel, with a thick ribbon of toothpaste oozing across the floor of his car, Gogarty hurried us out as fast as he could before racing off with his remaining victim to a date at a Dublin hospital.

The hotel people did welcome us. Because it was so late in September and out of season, we had what seemed to be a large, icy vault to ourselves. Sean had cherished his memories of Howth. Often he had told me how beautiful it was, but on this shivering day its beauties were lost on me until a fire had been lit and we had had tea and boiled eggs in front of it. Magically, the room was changed. So, when I looked from the window, was Howth. Then, as I remembered my pregnancy, the pleasure dwindled. Already I had taken various pills in an effort to lose the child; now I felt hemmed in and wanted urgently to be free. If I had longed so much to have Sean's child, why was I in such a state on our honeymoon? Was it (perhaps a convent inhibition?) because the child had been conceived before the marriage ceremony? Or did I grieve for my stage career? Whichever it was, that morning I was desperate.

During the next few days there was less time to think. We were busy travelling between Howth and Dublin, exploring Sean's favourite city, and seeing plays at the Abbey. As we had always to be limited by a suburban time-table, Sean said it would be more sensible to stay in Dublin itself, and we went to the Hotel Russell – at that time very simple – on St Stephen's Green. Living with Sean, I had begun to understand how much he suffered with his eyes and how patiently he endured it. Poverty in childhood had damaged his health; it never broke his will. Every morning, to relieve their pain, the eyes had to be bathed in very hot water, and fortunately at the Russell they brought up the jug regularly. Some hotels would have made a song about it.

Dr Joe Cummins, who had treated Sean's eyes in the old Dublin days, was still living in the dignity of Merrion Square.

Acutely anxious for me, Sean confided in him, and Cummins put us on to a leading gynaecologist who reassured me at once. I had in no way harmed the child or myself. It would be foolish not to continue. Immediately, and I suppose in character, I forgot all my worries, thought only of keeping healthy, and looked forward to the event. We both did. It had been our first emotional crisis, and it united us all the more.

The rest of that packed honeymoon stretched out for six weeks instead of the original fortnight. I saw many of Sean's friends, among them Barry Fitzgerald (the stage name of Will Shields) and Gabriel (Gaby) Fallon, who had been his 'butties'. I did wonder why Oliver Gogarty never asked us to his house. Maybe his wife was not forthcoming. I suspected snobbery there, though Sean had never noticed it and said wisely that, anyway, it didn't matter; Oliver did visit us more than once when we were in London and living at St John's Wood. I cannot recall that Sean met any of his relatives (as on our next trip he would). Though I was in touch with some of my Irish cousins in Mayo, Maynooth, and elsewhere, on a honeymoon neither of us gave relations more than a stray thought. One doesn't.

I kept up with Sunday Mass even if it was waning into a matter of habit. Sean would implore me to be in time, and I generally got in somehow to the 'late twelve' at the little church on St Stephen's Green, near the hotel; he would meet me at the end. I knew that I had been cheating for a long time: a Catholic is not meant to have love affairs. Why sex, the meeting of man and woman, should always be a principal sin, I never fathomed, but it was this that tortured you. You might believe, astonishingly, that after confession a load had been lifted; then back you had to go at once to your ordinary life and common failings. Sean was as reasonable about this as so much else.

We had no spare time. He wanted to show me everything in Dublin, his 'home of th' Ostmen, of th' Norman, and th' Gael', from the splendour of Phoenix Park to the Tara Brooch in the

National Museum. However impatient he might be at the waste
of intelligence, the impossibility (in 1927) of speaking one's
thoughts in Dublin's peculiar intellectual climate, he did profoundly love his city, its witty talk, the word-spinning of even
its poorest people. We did not forget the streets and tenements of
the *Gunman*, *Juno*, and the *Plough*; we drove out to Glendalough
in County Wicklow; we crossed the Silver Strand outside
Dublin, almost deserted in an October afternoon; and on our
last day we walked over the hill of Howth. Sean was telling me
of his work; his notebook was out more often. When again we
had reached the quay at Dun Laoghaire, the chill of that first
morning was forgotten; I, too, had come to love my birthplace.
Sean, happy about it all, was anxious none the less to return
to London – and to Dublin city as it would appear in the first
act of *The Silver Tassie*.

Sean O'Casey in 1927
Keogh Brothers, Dublin

Eileen O'Casey as a
Schoolgirl at the
Ursuline Convent,
Brentford

—and just before joining
The D'Oyly Carte Company
Brinkley & Son, Glasgow

In her modelling days
Janet Jevons

In her 30's—still on
the stage
Walter Bird

In the chorus of 'First Kiss', 1924. Eileen is second from the right
Ernest H. Mills

As a young mother with
Breon
Yevonde

CHAPTER NINE

Our First Home

SINCE my flat at St Andrew's Mansions was still let furnished –
though its tenants scorned the formality of paying rent – we
lived in Sean's first-floor flat at 32 Clareville Street. We ate our
meals, and he wrote, in the small sitting-room-study where he
had his divan and, under the window, his desk. We had, too, a
bedroom with another large divan; and a freezing bathroom
which had been a conservatory – it was like having a bath in
the middle of the Park. This was decidedly a one-man flat. I
had nowhere in it to hang my clothes, not even a mirror except
a cracked thing in the bathroom. We bought a chest and had
trays put into it, and I kept my clothes in that; and we did
get two mirrors, one long, the other oval.

As Sean had been there for a year before marriage I knew it
thoroughly. Yet it was strange to be living in the place together.
Ethel, a Cockney girl with bright red hair, came for a few
hours every morning to dust and polish and (after a fashion)
to get our breakfast. Previously Sean had given her the money
and let her carry on, which meant that daily she ordered a
standing supply of eggs and milk, and after a week had accumulated rations enough for a regiment. Inexperienced myself,
I took over what organising was needed. Sean had not married
a wife to take care of his money nor a housekeeper to take care
of his home. The most I did was to sew on a button or two and
mend his socks. My cooking had been basic, boiled eggs and the
pot of tea or jug of cocoa. Sean did go a bit beyond this. His
tea, I heard, was 'special' and his eggs were 'marvellous, done to

a turn'. He could also cook prunes and make a fair stew. Nothing slipshod: he would cook the prunes for the prescribed time and stand over them carefully while they were cooking. I never got to his stew, but he told me with pride what a hand he had been at it in Dublin. Tea-making was a separate rite: fresh water, heated pot, a great deal of tea, water added at the boil, and – this was vital – the concoction left for five minutes before it was poured and drunk. Result: a brew you could stand your spoon in, but it did you good.

Even in those early days, he had to rest in the afternoon for the sake of his eyes, lying with a handkerchief bandaged round his head. On most days he prepared for work towards evening and then wrote steadily. I had never been used to staying in at night; now it was a break to go out somewhere for an evening meal, and as often as not we dined at the Queen's. If we did stay in, any pair of girls living together extravagantly might have recognised our meal: I simply went to Harrods for expensive cold meats and salad. (Occasionally Sean did potatoes.)

Those first months of marriage slipped by like a holiday. The child dominated my ideas for the future. Sean had enough money to carry on; neither of us knew what saving meant, and we lived peacefully from week to week. Abbey Theatre cheques would arrive more or less regularly; as soon as the money was in the bank we drew it out. Sean kept the bank account, for I was hopeless here and my own account was what Maisie Madigan, in *Juno*, calls the Dublin police: null and void.

Mrs James, our landlady in Clareville Street, asked Sean if I would have a cup of tea with her one afternoon. Going obediently to her dark basement flat, I was received by several large cats in an Oriental-style room that smelt of cats and incense. Several tapers were burning; at a rapid glance I saw more cats sitting on the tops of bookcases and glaring at me. Noticing my fright, Mrs James said coaxingly, 'Pussy, nice pussy!' but the biggest nice pussy hardly budged, just slid a little nearer to gaze at me and dislike what he saw. Eyes everywhere, glowing in the tapers: very odd cats, over-petted, overfed. 'Now, my dear,' their mistress said to me, 'we must be friends . . . I can see into the future.' She was also, I gathered, a spiritualist. Generally I would be alert at any mention of the future or of fortune-telling, now I was too bemused to lift a finger. When Mrs James deserted the future to make tea, two or three of the cats lurched down and prowled out beside her. Others, malevolently inspecting me, remained on duty. I could scarcely muster a faint call. 'Mrs James,' I bleated, 'shall I help?' By this time she was back with the tea; I drank it as quickly as I could, told her I had promised Sean to go out, said goodbye, and fell upstairs to our own flat. I rarely saw her afterwards. She climbed up to us once a month to collect the rent; otherwise she seldom left her room. My terrier Bobby lived with us in Clareville Street for a while; if I had ever let him loose with those nice pussies he would have been totally submerged.

II

I have said that Christmas was not my favourite time. True, the year before, I had had a fresh experience with Helen and Yule Elliott, who invited me to Monte Carlo, where I gambled, had beginner's luck, bought a wildly expensive hat, and drove over the Riviera to Nice. There Lee was staying with his charming wife, a semi-invalid. Seeing them together forced me to think. I should have known then that our affair must end, though for all our tearful resolves to part we did see each other again in London. Now my first Christmas with Sean surprised me. What I had expected I cannot imagine, but I bought him a polo-necked sweater, wrapped it up, and gave it to him in the morning. Amazed, he had not considered presents himself; instead he suggested sensibly that it might be better if I went away to friends. I discovered that he had an urge to write: and gradually I learned that he never failed to work on festive occasions and Bank Holidays, a throwback to his years as a labourer when these were the only chances he had. Untroubled, I went to

Chalfont St Giles in Buckinghamshire. Mona Hilliam and Alison Gaunt were both living in the district; I spent Christmas with them and returned blissfully to Sean.

We were in entire harmony. While I was pregnant I would curl up sleepily on the divan, and Sean dreamt away and wrote. He was now drafting a play about the four seasons in Hyde Park which provisionally he called *The Green Gates*.

It was almost a shame to wake from our reverie. But Billy McElroy, anxious as usual, said we must have a larger home for ourselves and the child, not simply a two-roomed rented flat. Neither Chelsea nor Kensington appealed to me; I preferred north-west London, and in Woronzow Road, St John's Wood, near Primrose Hill and Regent's Park, we hit upon a little Georgian house with a ten-year lease – the preliminary deposit swallowed all the money Sean had. It was a friendly house. Its garden had matured; and in its huge kitchen was what Sean described as 'an old-fashioned range big enough to do as an altar for Stonehenge'. I was delighted, Sean semi-delighted. He hated moving though my own pleasure helped him. Since we had to begin with the furniture from Clareville Street, his own room rapidly took shape; it had a portable gas fire, but the grate was ready and Billy McElroy filled our cellar. To begin with, my room disappointed me. Its walls had been done in a very pale blue and I had a dark blue haircord carpet; the blend was a bit depressing. Moreover at first I had nothing but my divan and a flickering gas fire that hissed, popped, and spluttered.

Next, the tale of the bathroom, one of my special subjects. On our honeymoon I must have driven Sean half-crazy. So many of the baths were peculiar. At Howth you got out stained like a relief map by the chipped enamel. In the Dublin hotel scalding hot water gushed from both taps. In London it was a skirmish to get from that polar bathroom-conservatory in Clareville Street to the warm bedroom. Inspecting Woronzow Road, I said to myself that it would be luxurious to have a small bathroom off my bedroom, usual in America, rare still in Britain. Until we could change it, our old bathroom was not for loiterers, its walls in a bilious green, a scrap of worn oilcloth on the floor. An ancient brass geyser spluttered like my bedroom fire; the bath, which was large and serviceable, was in enamel with a plain wooden surround. One evening towards the end of my pregnancy, while Sean was in his room chatting to Billy McElroy, I got ready for a bath and took in matches with me to light the pilot jet which had blown out. The next second a fierce explosion blew window, frame and all, into the street; everywhere glass was splintered. Billy, rushing to investigate, saw only chaos crusted with black dirt that had erupted from the geyser. It was more than he could take. After a single glance he made for the front door, shouting over his shoulder as he ran downstairs, 'I'm afraid, Sean, I won't be any help here.'

Sean cried after him, 'You're a fine friend, I must say!' Muttering to himself, 'What a thing for a man to do!' he telephoned the doctor. I was unhurt as it happened; and Sean was more concerned that Billy had run off. 'Do you know,' he said over the cup of tea essential in an emergency, 'Do you know, I don't think I'm ever going to see or talk to that fellow again.' Billy's conscience must have been dire. He telephoned later that night, and I heard Sean say, 'Well, that's perfectly all right . . . but I still can't understand why you ran away.' I guessed that relations would be restored, and they were. Sean next day was in his 'Nothing happened at all' mood. Several people asked what the trouble had been, but since nothing was wrong with me it was simpler to forget. With the insurance money we made an excellent new bathroom. Billy came round as usual.

I think it was during these early days of marriage that Ben invited us to lunch with him and a friend who had something to do with a famous make of bullet-proof glass. The friend loved Sean's plays and the right sort of theatre – to Ben it was merely an amusement. Our rendezvous, off Piccadilly, was one of London's most fashionable restaurants, a dark, secluded place with four steps down to the bar and dining-room as you entered. Sean was afraid he would take a header. 'I can't see a damned thing,' he whispered. Once downstairs, we had almost to feel our path to the table; Sean certainly did, and when we were seated in the encircling gloom, he muttered again, 'And now I won't be able to see a damned thing I'm eating.' I was careful that he chose a simple dish. In the darkness talk did begin to flow, and when at length we extricated ourselves to say good-bye, blinking in the daylight, we all shook hands heartily. Sean and Ben never met again, and on that occasion they had seen very little of each other.

III

Before we bought our other essential furniture, I had taken Sean to Charing Cross Road to hunt for prints. We were days choosing them – Van Gogh, Renoir, many impressionists – and we could have gone on much longer. Heals next, for carpets and curtains; we sat, the small matter of money forgotten, with patterns piled round us and the salesman persuaded that we were a couple of eccentric millionaires. Sean, peering closely at colours and materials, promptly chose the most expensive. I was extravagant – or possibly regardless. It was good to get the home together and not to care a damn about saving. Billy, in a half-demented moment, had proposed that I should open an account – no trouble for me because I had plenty of the best references. My taste was simple, but simplicity can cost a lot, and so it did now.

We must have been camping in Woronzow Road for a month or five weeks before I could get my own furniture from St Andrew's Mansions. The tenants had flitted to Australia and left the flat in an appalling state, but I did have two bedroom suites, one of walnut, one of oak, with dining- and sitting-room furniture, crockery, china, and an upright Bechstein piano. With all this the house suddenly filled up. It was bright with our coloured prints; and Sean had an enchanting picture, the head of a *gitana*, that he had bought at an Augustus John exhibition. He wrote to Lady Gregory: 'We have six originals now, and some beautiful prints by modern artists. We have declared war on the clumsy, gaudy, garish, picture-degrading cult of gilt framing, and enclosed them all in simple oak, walnut, or ebony frames.'

Everything was ready in time. We lived our own lives by day and went out at night. Bernard Shaw's 'pentateuch', *Back to Methuselah*, had begun a Court Theatre revival, and the part we chose started at six o'clock with a dinner-break midway. By now I was enormous. Finding it awkward to keep my shoes on, I kicked both of them off during the play; at the interval, when we were ready to go across the square to dine at the Queen's, the shoes had vanished. Sean was most embarrassed, but we spotted them down near the orchestra. What made it worse was that my feet had swollen to twice their size. It was impossible to get the wretched things on again. Somehow I hobbled from theatre to restaurant, Sean murmuring, 'For the Lord's sake, dear, try to keep them on during dinner, or we'll never get back to the theatre.' In the second half I did take them off and held them carefully on my lap. Later, not a chance: I went shoeless from the theatre, and we had to hail a taxi home.

One afternoon, when I was at an Earls Court fair with Alison Gaunt, I consulted a fortune-teller. She hardly needed to be clever to see that I was having a child: I only just fitted into her tent. But she did tell me that I would have some great misfortune. 'Anyone could have told you about the child,' Sean said gloomily. 'It serves you right, Eileen, if you *will* listen to such nonsense. Anyhow, don't worry about it.'

A month before the baby was due, I had arranged to go to the theatre. That afternoon Dr Harold Waller warned me to drop the idea; he would like to bring in a specialist and maybe induce the birth. Though the cot Helen had ordered for us was not ready, the firm agreed to lend us one, and in an hour or so it was delivered, a white cot touched here and there with gold paint. Dear Mrs Earle, who was with me, exclaimed, 'Darling. doesn't it look like a coffin!' 'Don't say that!' I cried, 'Don't say that!' and immediately I thought of the fortune-teller. In the evening the specialist arrived; because it would be a com-

plicated birth, and at home, the doctors felt it would be best for
Sean to go away for the night. They also told him that, in
emergency, he might have to choose between us – myself or the
baby. Unhesitatingly, he chose me. Off he went to Billy
McElroy's while Mrs Earle and a nurse remained in the house.

On the next morning, a lovely, glowing April day, Sean heard
than our first child, a boy who would be called Breon, had been
born during the early hours. When he had hurried back to
Woronzow Road to see me, and was just about to go upstairs,
he noticed among his letters on the hall table one from Dublin.
This must be the answer from the Abbey. He opened it and read
W. B. Yeats's rejection of *The Silver Tassie*. They did not want
the play: 'You have no subject . . . You are not interested in
the Great War.' Sean was utterly shocked; for many minutes
he must have sat in silence on the stair. Yet it was a week before I heard anything about it. That day he came up and em-
braced me, he was excited to see Breon, and he kept the Abbey
refusal to himself, doing nothing to damage the wonderful,
serene morning with the lilac trees in bloom beyond my window.

IV

A lot has been written about the rejection of *The Silver Tassie*
but not, I think, a syllable too much. We know today what it
did. Yeats, who was primarily responsible, removed a great
dramatist from the Irish theatre. I believe myself that it was
largely jealousy. After almost fifty years we are aware what an
achievement the *Tassie* was, especially at that bleak time. With
its second act abandoning realism for speech superbly height-
ened, it is a great play still.

Yeats's action injured Sean financially. If it had not been for
C. B. Cochran's courage as a manager, and the influential
opinion of G.B.S. and others, his whole future would have been
imperilled. Yeats was the leading Irish poet; people would have
followed his opinion and assumed he was right. I am convinced

that, but for this, the later plays would have been staged without question. To Sean, who had respected Yeats down the years, it was betrayal. Badly hurt, he was grateful for a closer friend's insistent support. 'What a hell of a play!' G.B.S. wrote in a letter, and he repeated his enthusiasm ('Cheerio, Titan!') over luncheon in Whitehall Court. There was other powerful help. Sean, using the third person, would write in the fifth volume of his autobiography, *Rose and Crown*:

[He] carried the letters of Yeats to . . . Mr Daniel Macmillan, remarking that if the Firm wished, after reading them, he would allow the contract to be withdrawn. Mr Daniel read the correspondence through. He handed it back to Sean, saying, This is, of course, a matter between Mr Yeats and you. It does not concern us. We do not agree with the criticism. We think the play worth publication, and we will publish it. We make our own decisions, and this controversy cannot alter our intentions.

Very kind, very manly, and very encouraging to Sean, for he had had a half fear that the criticism from Yeats might check, might even prevent, the play's publication. This was his first victory over the potent, almost impregnable influence of Yeats.

There had to be one further disappointment. Sir Barry Jackson drove up to Woronzow Road in June 1928 to tell us that, though the *Tassie* was among the finest new plays he had ever read, it was too frightening for him to stage. Here was a sensitive man with respect for another artist's feelings. Unlike the people of the Abbey, Barry Jackson was brave enough to say in person what he genuinely regretted.

As it was, it would be sixteen months before the *Tassie* reached the London theatre. Sean, concentrating on *Within the Gates* (final name of the Hyde Park play), had enough to do. The plan had been growing since he moved to Clareville Street; he wanted, he said, 'to bring back to the drama the music and song and dance of the Elizabethan play and the austere ritual of the

Greek drama, caught up and blended with the life around us.'
The Park, the orators at Speakers' Corner, the whole existence
of the region – a republic on its own – had fascinated him. A
few of the speakers, one a volubly eloquent atheist, called on us
in Woronzow Road; and we met a young prostitute, an educated, attractive girl who was a friend of Augustus John, and
whom Sean encouraged to describe her life, how she had drifted
into it, how she found her regular clients.

v

I had settled down with Sean, but I had not really settled into
marriage. Mrs Earle came in daily to keep house: I was not
concerned with the running of the place or what we had for
meals; indeed it would be seven years before I accepted my home
and its details as my principal interest. To take care of Breon –
though I was with him myself constantly – I had engaged
Nanny Trim, a tiny, rather plain but warm and loving country-
woman. The theatre did linger in my mind. Still, I had not
thought seriously of going back to it until a wholly unprepared
talk with C. B. Cochran.

Bravest of managers, always prepared to follow his instinct,
he had begun with a 'quiet, strange, and mysterious influence',
as Sean put it, to collect his backing for The Silver Tassie. On
a tranquil Sunday in the early summer of 1929 we drove down
to a cottage the Cochrans had rented in the Thames Valley.
Most of the afternoon Sean and C.B. were discussing the play
with Raymond Massey, the Canadian actor who would direct
it. Then Cochran beckoned me aside. 'Eileen,' he said, 'you must
return to the stage.'

I had not considered much beyond my daily life with Sean
and Breon. But C.B. was wise. He wondered what my feelings
might be when the excitement of having Breon had worn off
and I was alone at night while Sean was writing and the house
was very quiet. The evenings had been my special world. Sean

himself, Cochran said, would like me to get back to the theatre. Might it not hurt him if I grew bored and discontented? There was much to ponder. It did not surprise me when, a few weeks later, C.B. invited me to audition for a new musical play. I went along and was offered a part as one of six young Victorian bridesmaids who would reappear as society matrons. The author, composer, and director was Noël Coward, and the 'operette' was called *Bitter Sweet*.

CHAPTER TEN

Bitter Sweet

Bitter Sweet was to open at His Majesty's, but its rehearsals in June 1929 were on the wide stage of the Scala, up behind Tottenham Court Road, a theatre since pulled down. During the first week among that gilt and marble it puzzled me why others in the company had received their contracts and I had not. There seemed no reason to leave me out, but who could say what might be going on in the background? Every day I asked for my contract; regularly Cochran told me not to worry. But I did worry, and I could not help noticing a girl who was hanging round in the wings; instinct told me she was not there for the fun of it.

Nothing really registered until Cochran said one morning – and I am sure he was relieved – 'You can go and get your contract now, Eileen. And would you like to have lunch with me?' Clearly he had a reason, and I soon heard what it was: Noël Coward, who liked my work at rehearsal, had been shy of having me in the cast when he realised that Eileen Carey was Mrs Sean O'Casey. Even when he agreed that I was suitable, I kept on asking myself what the trouble could be, for Noël and Sean, so far as I knew, had not visited each other. Sean suggested that it all went back to his first year in London. He was succeeding with *Juno* and the *Plough*; and Noël, most prolific of the young English dramatists and author of *The Vortex* and *Hay Fever*, had written for an opinion on his own work. Whereupon Sean had replied, candidly but perhaps naïvely in the circumstances, that the early plays had been good but he would do better if he went more deeply into his characters. If this had annoyed the ambitious young man of the twenties, I must say that as soon as he had accepted me in *Bitter Sweet*, he never hinted at any dislike. To me he was an ideal director. I was glad that I had known nothing during those preliminary rehearsals; if I had I might have done badly from sheer nervous strain.

The play was a romantic 'operette': Coward held that it was the moment for a romantic revival. Beginning and ending in a Belgrave Square mansion at the present day, most of it flashed back to three nineteenth-century scenes and to the story of the girl who eloped with her Austrian music master; after only five years she saw him killed in a duel while he was defending her honour in a Viennese café. Noël had included several of his most haunting songs, 'If Love Were All,' the 'Green Carnations' quartet, 'Zigeuner' ('Play to me beneath the summer moon'), and the famous 'I'll See You Again' which set London humming:

> I'll see you again
> Whenever Spring breaks through again;
> Time may lie heavy between,
> But what has been
> Is past forgetting.

Peggy Wood, the American actress, came to play the leading part.

Bitter Sweet began a good three months before Cochran's production of *The Silver Tassie*. In July 1929 we opened for a fortnight in Manchester where everything sailed along – the London run appeared to be secure. On the day of the première at His Majesty's Sean was writing this letter to Lady Gregory at her country house in County Galway:

> 19 Woronzow Road,
> St John's Wood,
> 18 July 1929.

Dear Lady Gregory,

Thanks for your letter and its core of kind remembrance.

I'm fairly well, though my health hasn't been always easy,

and my eyes trouble me a good deal. But these are things that
entrenched themselves in me in childhood, and the only thing
to do is to fight a defensive war and keep them under cover.
Anyhow I have often been worse, and as I have married a
splendid girl in every way, and as we are very happy together,
a girl who has never tired me for a moment, whose good
taste in pictures is remarkable, and who is quickly acquiring
one for good books, and who is a great mother – then I have
many reasons indeed for believing that the goodness of God
hasn't altogether left me alone. We lead a very simple life, and
the difficulties of meeting our needs – for we have been faced
with the fact of having none to spare – have brought us
closer together. She has a part in *Bitter Sweet* to be produced
tonight here, which will, perhaps, gather a few pounds together for herself and her particular needs.

Our little plantation is beautiful too, full of delphiniums,
lupins, petunias, pansies, dahlias, and peonies, and the apples
on two trees we have are getting very fat and important-
looking ...

II

The London opening of *Bitter Sweet* began in disappointment.
Cochran, we recognised, was a genius at advertising and at
thrusting a show forward; yet when we left the stage door that
night, most of us felt strangely deflated, though less, possibly,
than Noël himself who said that the house had reminded him of
'cornflour blancmange'. Another call for rehearsal was
ominous. Still, Cochran persisted. No one lost heart. At the end
of the week a play to which some critics had given three months,
and which Sean did not like, was moving into a hit. By October,
with everything set for the complex production of the *Tassie* at
the Apollo in Shaftesbury Avenue, *Bitter Sweet* was so entrenched that it ran for almost two years.

Once we had begun, I was peaceful. I was living a professional woman's life in my own sphere while Sean was safe in his. The theatre at night for me; for him the prospect of the *Tassie* in performance, and the steady growth of *Within the Gates*. We had local moments of domestic comedy. During the preparations for *Bitter Sweet*, Cochran urged me to come to a party. Sean, I said, might not like it, but C.B. insisted; his guests, I fancy, were theatre backers and he particularly wanted me. So I dolled up and went. It was an average party: dinner and dancing, and (though I had lost much of my zest for it) a fair amount of flirting. When I returned about three or four in the morning, Sean was still up. He met me in silence, and, furious at his manner, I told him that I had been through a frightful evening for the theatre's sake and it was outrageous that he could be either jealous or annoyed. At breakfast next morning he sulked. I was bright enough, prepared to describe the party; from Sean not a word. I put up with it until the end of the meal, then I snatched up the marmalade jar and threw it at him; it fell on his lap and a little was spilt. Wiping the fragments off the chair in dignified silence, he rose, observed, 'That was an extraordinary thing for you to do, Eileen,' and left. Presently I went to his room, ready to yell. Were we going to take a vow of eternal silence because for once I had stayed out late? I found him roaring with laughter, so we kissed and made it up. Quarrels have their points: making up is a joy.

III

Cochran pressed ahead with *The Silver Tassie*. He hoped that Augustus John, who had done no scenic work for the theatre, might design the second act in the War Zone. Sean's description would challenge any artist: the 'jagged and lacerated ruins of what was once a monastery'; a lighted stained-glass window; a life-size crucifix; and, in the midst, the big howitzer and its 'long, sinister barrel' that pointed towards the Front; 'every feature of the scene a little distorted from its original appearance'. Cochran asked me to suggest it to Augustus, who was a loyal friend. Generously, as a wedding gift, he had presented us with the portrait of Sean that hung over our mantelpiece; but to beg this particular favour needed courage. However, I telephoned, went to tea at Augustus's studio in Mallord Street, Chelsea, and at last heard him say, 'Well, yes, Eileen . . . I will do it for you and Sean, and I hope I manage it.' Indeed, he managed it, though scene-shifters would have trouble with his wonderful and overpowering set, it was so heavily built.

Cochran took infinite care with the *Tassie* company. Sean had been anxious that his old 'buttie', Barry Fitzgerald, creator of the Paycock, should play Sylvester Heegan, who has that early speech about the night when his son Harry 'punched the fear of God into the heart of Police Constable 63 C under the stars of a frosty night on the way home from Terenure':

> An' the hedges by the road-side standin' stiff in the silent cold of the air, the frost beads on the branches glistenin' like toss'd-down diamonds from the breasts of the stars, the quiet-ness of the night stimulated to a fuller stillness by the mockin' breathin' of Harry, an' the heavy, ragin' pantin' of the Bobby, and the quickenin' beats of our own hearts afraid of hopin' too little or hopin' too much.

Fitzgerald was duly engaged; Beatrix Lehmann and Binnie Barnes were the girls; and for the central figure, Harry Heegan, the Dublin footballer who returns from the war paralysed from the waist downward, C.B. fixed on Charles Laughton. Sean was uncertain. Most discussed of the young actors, Laughton was never easy. Imaginatively in tune with the part, he was un-suited physically to a tall man 'with the sinewy muscles of a manual worker made flexible by athletic sport'.

The night was 11 October 1929. Objecting to any inter-ference with his casts, Cochran was not disposed to let me off *Bitter Sweet*. We pleaded successfully, and in a box at the Apollo that night, I sat with him and his wife Evelyn during three hours of strong emotion. Sean himself was somewhere inconspicuous at the back of the theatre. Generously, G.B.S. went to find him between the second and third acts and to re- assure him again that it was a great play. On the following morning, when Cochran sent up the notices to Woronzow Road, Sean read how the *Tassie* had fought itself free from the Abbey disaster. The reception had been terrific. He wrote in *Rose and Crown*:

> Up went the London curtain on *The Silver Tassie*, and, in spite of the fact that Laughton was badly miscast, and had a bad cold, that a few others were as bad as he, in spite of a few mishaps, the play was a hit; not at all in the conventional sense, but in a moral and a complex sense; using a Joxerian expression, the play gave the patient, wondering public a terrible belt in the kisser . . . It tried to go into the heart of war, and, to many people whom it blasted with dismay, it succeeded.

Sean had not forgiven the people of the Abbey. This showed when he refused to see Lady Gregory, who was in London, and who wrote asking if she might meet his wife and child. Sean's early encourager, she had been far more of a friend than Yeats. It did not help her now. Her implicit association with Yeats's refusal had wounded Sean. I was most upset that he would not receive her. Though at heart he wanted it, he was too stubborn. 'Bitterness', he wrote to her, 'would certainly enter into things I would say about W. B. Yeats and L. Robinson if we were to meet, bitterness that would hurt you, and I am determined to avoid hurting you as much as possible.' She wrote to him twice while she was in London, and in her second letter (23 October 1929) she said: 'Although I missed the pleasure of seeing you, I should like to tell you what I have just written to Yeats about the *Tassie* – "I am troubled because, having seen the play, I believe we ought to have accepted it. We could not have done the chanted scene as it is done here, it is very fine and im- pressive." – But I say and think we could have done the other acts better – Barry Fitzgerald was, of course, very fine.' Sean

had loved her dearly. It was an example of the manner in which
one can hurt both the person one loves, and oneself, because of
a stubborn refusal to forgive. Then forgiveness can come too
late. Sean wrote (again in the third-person manner of his autobiography):

> Eileen begged him to change his mind, saying his refusal to
> see her would hurt Lady Gregory more than anything he
> might say. But, no; he would not let her come . . . This re-
> fusal was one of his silly sins. He still thinks angrily of him-
> self when he thinks of her, or hears the name of the gracious,
> gallant woman. He should have listened to Eileen . . .

IV

From now onwards, until May 1931, my evenings were spent at
the theatre. I shared a dressing-room at His Majesty's with three
of the six bridesmaids: Maie Drage (Harriet), who I think had
appeared only with D'Oyly Carte; Mary Pounds (Effie), daughter of the tenor, Courtice Pounds (who had been in *The First
Kiss*); and Rose Hignell (Gloria), who had been a *Beggar's Opera*
Polly and who was understudying Peggy Wood. She had a
romance of long standing with an equerry at Buckingham
Palace, an exciting half-secret; when they were to meet, the
dressing room was in turmoil – no one could get near our only
small basin. Maie was engaged to the later Sir Hardman Earle.
Mary's permanent boy-friend had a house on the river and
bred dogs. We enjoyed meeting at night. Mary was a very good
bridge player, so we joined in what I called 'dressing-room
bridge'. Hands were dealt; everyone dwelt seriously on trumps
or whatever (I could never enter into it fully myself), and at the
tensest moment the talk would begin.

> 'Did any of you see that wonderful dress in that Shaftesbury
> Avenue shop today?'

'Which shop?'
'Oh, about halfway up on the right.'

That was the cue for a long description of the dress and everything about it until Mary would throw down her hand, crying, 'Look here, it's quite impossible to play with any of you.' And for a while there would be a subdued silence.

We always talked over any problems we might have. As we were on in only the first and third acts, we could often have something to eat in our room; Mac, my dresser, who belonged to the Cochran company, would bring coffee and sandwiches. By day, too, we saw a good bit of each other; the girls would call at Woronzow Road, especially when I was looking after Breon, and either Maie or Rose would go with us to Regent's Park. I had also got to know Peggy Wood, whose son David and Breon were much the same age. She was a most intelligent girl, married at the time to Johnnie Weaver, a young American poet. When she arrived to rehearse *Bitter Sweet* she was in tweeds and looking far less glamorous than the usual run of leading ladies, but at the dress rehearsal we were overwhelmed by her beauty, dignity, and grace.

It was a busy week: a performance every night and two matinées. On non-matinée days one had to get ready about six o'clock. Having lost my old trick of tearing about in taxis, I used a bus that stopped at the end of our road and went conveniently past His Majesty's in the Haymarket, and if Sean met me after the show we could catch the last bus home. Not much like those *Rose Marie* days when I would roll up to Drury Lane in a taxi or Helen's Daimler.

Frequently, between Saturday shows, the girls in our dressing-room would go to the downstairs grill-room at the Regent Palace. Three of us, Rose, Maie, and myself, were there one evening. After our meal – steak, pudding, all of it – we found when they brought the bill that we could raise about ten shillings between us, no more. Panic set in. Dreadfully late already, we rushed over to the desk and explained that we had come from His

Majesty's Theatre. They looked blank. A new manager did not know us from a hole in the wall, and we stared frantically around without seeing a friend. How could the young ladies settle the bill? Had we any valuables? Anything we might leave? No, hardly anything. The manager remained dour. Time went by. As a last gamble we told him to ring C. B. Cochran, and probably the mere sound of the name was enough for us, for as soon as we heard it spoken we tore together from the restaurant, dashed down Haymarket, reached our stage door at the last minute of the last hour, and got on just in time. Only those who have worked in the theatre can appreciate our fright. To miss the curtain, or to have it held, was the ultimate crime: we would have lost our jobs, lost everything. Yet we had made it. The restaurant people who had pursued us to the theatre got no further – the stage doorkeeper saw to that. Half an hour passed before Cochran himself arrived at the theatre in one of his stateliest moods. We had been doubly to blame, irresponsible about our obligations to the company and about the use of his name in public. Ready to reprimand me, he saw that I was in tears, trying to tell him what had happened. Mercifully, in time, he began to laugh. 'When you go next, Eileen,' he said, 'have either enough money on you or enough jewellery.' It had been far too close a thing for us all.

V

As I recall it, the late summer of 1930 was very hot. During a long run one forgets a holiday, but Nanny Trim was accustomed to families who took them at the proper time. Other nannies she met in the Park would soon be off to one spot or another and she believed that Breon should be getting sea air. Previously we had been to Angmering. Now she told us of a Margate address from one of her former posts, so I booked our lodgings, Sean left with Nanny and Breon, and I travelled down myself at the week-end, arriving in the small hours, sleeping at a tiny hotel because there was no room in the digs, and staying until Monday afternoon. Sean enjoyed mooning about the crowded beach and listening to the people. The digs were comfortable, in the evening the landlady gave him a coal fire, and he could get through his work unfussed. Nanny Trim was never in the way. Night by night I spoke to him on the telephone; Mrs Earle would sleep with me in Woronzow Road, and it was only when she had to get back to her family that I felt lost.

Most writers work at home. Sean could be unsettled when no one was around; the tenement noises had been a part of his youth. As a child I was always one of a mob, rarely with more than half an hour to myself, and I still like company. If anybody is in the house I work on untroubled; if alone I must force myself not to waste time. Now, in Sean's absence at Margate, I was glad to go out to supper – with Geoffrey Carte maybe, or Doctor Waller. One night, to my astonishment, who should turn up at the stage door but Lee! It was only a business visit, something to do with casting, and not especially to see me, but his mere presence was fatal. Without Sean's protective influence it was irresistible to accept an invitation. Gradually, emotions revived. Two or three times we saw each other, visiting places we had known and getting back to an almost forgotten rhythm. When, on a moonlit night, he proposed that we should drive out into the country, the inevitable happened.

He went off to America. Imagining we had met for the last time, I said nothing about this to Sean. If it had been anyone but Lee I might have done; here I was more than usually secretive. Complications never occurred to me. Then, startled, I found I was pregnant and had to tell Sean that the child was not his. At once, he guessed.

Without seeing him again I left for the theatre; he had been badly shaken. How I got through I shall never know: I dreaded the return to Woronzow Road. Just as I was asking the stage doorkeeper to call me a cab, he said, 'Mr O'Casey is already in a taxi waiting for you.' I threw myself into Sean's arms. His love and understanding at that moment are indelible; but the worry had made me so ill that a Harley Street specialist ordered an operation, and after the Saturday performance I was driven at midnight to a nursing-home. Within a week I was back at work. Sean never mentioned it again, treating it solely as a matter between ourselves.

VI

In lesser matters you could not be sure. Nanny Trim and Breon had made friends in Regent's Park with a nanny and child from a house in Avenue Road five minutes away from us. Now and again I had tea with the parents, and they invited me to come one evening to a dance and supper in their garden. Telling Sean I would not be late, I went straight to the party from the theatre, forgot the time, came to at four in the morning, and begged an urgent lift home. There the lights were full on in the hall and sitting-room. Sean, who was singing to himself, greeted me cheerfully. 'Well, dear, I've had a glass of wine. You see I can be as gay as you are.' This was better than silence. I told him where I had been, and he sat contentedly, his arms round me. He seldom drank anything, and a single glass of wine could make him quite merry.

Good; but there could be other moods. One afternoon while I was off, ill, the stage doorkeeper telephoned for instructions. What should he do with the flowers for Miss Eileen Carey?

'Flowers?' asked Sean. 'What flowers?'

'Oh, the usual ones, sir. They come for her quite often.'

Send them to a hospital, Sean told him, or give them to Miss Carey's friends. Upset, he hurried to see me. I had to explain that a man who had been to every *Bitter Sweet* matinée for a year had formed the habit of sending flowers round to me with a note; over tea at the Carlton Hotel I had warned him that I was married, with a child. It was nothing more than the common over-the-footlights 'crush', and I said firmly to Sean, 'Don't you understand why I didn't tell you?' I had no intention of suffering days of silence, and probably a scene, for an incident so trivial. By then *Bitter Sweet* was ending and I heard no more.

Though by now it seemed to have grown into our lives, the play could not be expected to continue indefinitely. After practically two years it had been transferred to the Palace Theatre and – with an intervening week or so at Golders Green – to the Lyceum at cheaper prices, and with Evelyn Laye instead of Peggy Wood. The Lyceum run was brief, a bare month; and in May 1931 the company dispersed.

I was faced now with the problem Cochran had described on that summer afternoon. No trouble by day; I was occupied with the house and with Breon and Sean. But about eight in the evening when Sean was alone with his work, and Breon asleep, I became increasingly restless and frustrated. (To this day, at eight o'clock, I feel that somewhere a curtain must be rising and I should be there.) I can never read a book until bedtime. I am not a pianist. After the convent, needlework had bored me. At Woronzow Road, and at an hour when I should have been out and about, it was impossible – as Cochran had foreseen – to adjust myself to the stillness. More than this, we were living past our means. Sean had had no new play since the *Tassie* which ran for only two months. All the money we had I had spent as it came in, mostly on furnishings and carpets, the making of a home. And as Sean said in *Rose and Crown*:

The Income Tax Collector, a kindly man, was coming to the house on the track of fifty pounds owed to the Revenue, which sum Sean hadn't got, but which the Collector thought must be found somewhere. Sean had tried to interest the kindly man in the bees in the garden, but the Collector didn't care about bees. He said he didn't know a thing about them; how they lived, or how they were brought up, or a ha'porth. He knew a bee could sting a man, but that was about all. He was glad to hear they were so useful to man in the pollination of flowers, a thing he hadn't known before. He knew, of course, that bees were thrifty things, laying up a store for a rainy day, and so a lesson to us all. He had other calls to make, but hoped he'd get the fifty pounds before the weekend, for he couldn't wait indefinitely, and went his way.

Book-buying aside, Sean was never extravagant. At Woronzow Road he was happy. Even if his heart was in his own room where he had all he asked, books, fire, typewriter, armchair, and divan, he loved to roam out into the rest of the house we had so long talked about and planned. It was wearily apparent that we could not go on as we were. Regretfully, and not knowing what else to do, we sold the remainder of our lease.

Billy McElroy bobbed up again, as he had done so often. His daughter, he said, had a cottage at Chalfont St. Giles; she might rent it to us. He continued to be an influence, so we accepted the idea. With real heartbreak we had to part with Mrs Earle and Nanny Trim (Breon was three years old and getting too much for her), and arranged to put our furniture into store. I found a girl called Tessa who would be able, I thought, to stay with Breon if, as I hoped, I went on working in the theatre. That was all. Sadly, in the autumn of 1931, we said goodbye to the one house we would ever own.

As one of the bridesmaids (on the far left) in 'Bitter Sweet'
Sacha

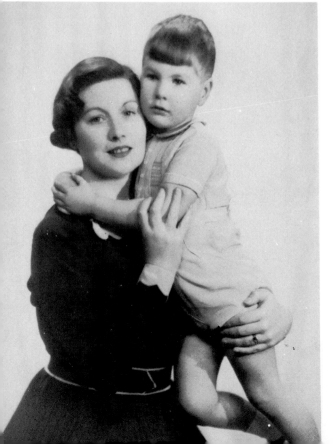

With her second son,
Niall
Elwin Neame

Eileen with Shivaun at Totnes in 1940

The family being filmed for NBC at Torquay
l. to r. Robert Emmett Ginna, Sean, Breon, Eileen, Niall and Shivaun
Suschitzky

The grandchildren—
Shivaun with Ruben
Julian Neiman

Breon and Doreen's
children—top to bot-
tom, Oona, Duibhne
and Brendan
Ander Gunn, Penzance

Eileen as she is now

CHAPTER ELEVEN

I Leave the Stage

THE change was certainly bleak. From the relative luxury of
St John's Wood, we landed at Chalfont (Milton's Chalfont,
though who cared about that?) and a workman's cottage barely
modernised: four rooms, two up, two down, with a straight
staircase between them, a bathroom that was a long drop from
Woronzow Road, and an outside lavatory that was at least
under cover. We had a pleasant strip of front lawn; in three
weeks of deceptively fine weather we began by quite liking the
place. Sean wrote away at the first volume of his autobiography,
I Knock at the Door, about his Dublin childhood ('swift glances
back at things that made me'). We walked miles through the
Chiltern lanes, at times with the push-chair, at others leaving
Breon to the girl Tessa, while Sean, telling me eagerly about his
earliest youth, would get his memories organised. Each of us
had a quick sense of fun; being a descriptive talker myself, I
would reply with my own stories, everything that had been
happening to me. In those first weeks, like a holiday almost, we
got home at tea-time and had an hour or so with Breon. All very
well; but as the holiday spirit weakened, we wondered what on
earth could have brought us to Chalfont St Giles. Sean could not
have gone on working in a cottage lighted only by oil-lamps. His
eyesight was so poor that even when we put a second lamp
in the sitting-room, he could not make his longhand draft
with ease unless he lay upon the floor with the lamps beside him.

The cottage was on a large estate. Its owner, who called on

us now and then, never found Sean very forthcoming, and we did not return the visits. At this season, the ebb of summer, the Chiltern country and its trees looked beautiful; and by some act of self-hypnotism – how else I cannot say – we persuaded ourselves that we really did want to stay in the country. With rents so much lower than those in London, we might sensibly get some other house and go on experimenting. That was what we did. One day we were taken over Hillcrest, an agreeable bungalow inexpensive to rent; it had an orchard behind it, and in front a large garden that an old man tended for the owners. The lease, three months on each side, was undemanding, so hopefully we took the furniture out of store and cut up our carpets and curtains to suit the bungalow. Billy McElroy filled our cellar; Sean chose a little room at the back – a squash but, after a bit of juggling, set up on his invariable pattern – and I began resolutely to see about another job.

Though my conscience fretted me about Breon and Sean, I was emotionally unsettled, still thinking of my career. Sean supported me. He was a stoic of stoics. He had never stopped his creative work, whatever the opposition, and for my sake and Breon's he was ready to put up as best he could with these miseries of suburban life in the country.

II

In the spring of 1932 Barry Jackson revived Rutland Boughton's Celtic-myth opera, The Immortal Hour, at the Queen's Theatre. Asked to audition for the chorus, I sang a fairly serious ballad before seeing in alarm that we were to have a sight-reading test. Luckily, for sight-reading was never one of my talents, they called in five or six of us to do the same piece; even more luckily, I was fifth in the queue, and by close listening, and with a little artistic hesitation, I did all they required. The job fixed, and resolved to get home from it whenever possible, I found rooms within reach of both the Metropolitan Railway and the Green

Line bus stop at Marble Arch; it was an hour's bus ride almost
to our door. During rehearsal only week-ends were possible;
during the run I could leave London at ten in the morning and
stay until four at Chalfont.

This *Immortal Hour* chorus was unlike others I had known;
there were few of us and most of the girls had been trained at
major academies. Our chorus-master, an expert musician, directed the entire rehearsals. When the show was running, and he
needed that far-off effect in 'How beautiful they are, the lordly
ones!' he would begin to conduct us while going down the
stairs to the stage, and so forward into the wings where we
continued to sing for the rest of the scene. We ran for six weeks.
By the fourth I had fallen in love with our conductor. Several
of us had been used to having coffee or a drink together, but
now I went to supper with him on most evenings, to a simple
Italian restaurant in Soho or any place good and inexpensive. At
the week-end I confessed to Sean that I had fallen desperately
in love. He listened patiently. 'Eileen, dear,' he said at length,
'I don't think this man would be any good to you. It doesn't
sound as though he has any steady money. He doesn't sound a
steady fellow in any way. I'm not worried . . . I'm sure you will
soon forget him.' As usual he was right. Back in London I found
the man's attraction was dwindling, and when the show had
ended I never gave him another thought.

III

As soon as *The Immortal Hour* was over, Cochran sent me to
audition for the chorus of *The Miracle*. It was another revival
but a vast one: the 'wordless mystery spectacle' based on Pro-
vençal legend, and with Humperdinck's music, which Cochran
put on in a production by Reinhardt. Twenty years before this
they had done it on an immense scale at Olympia. Now the
stage of the Lyceum Theatre became a cathedral, a setting which
was extended to cover the boxes by the proscenium. We had a

chorus of nearly two hundred, mostly singing up in the gallery by the orchestra, and the cast, with such people in it as Lyn Harding and the former dancer Maud Allan, contained 'Mr Cochran's Young Ladies' (Eileen Carey among them) and a number of society amateurs. Lady Diana Cooper repeated her almost legendary performance of the Madonna, a statue that came to life in place of a nun who deserted her convent and returned after many years; Tilly Losch was the girl. Altogether, an experience in that incense-filled theatre; I remember our rushes from stage to gallery and back, and the personality of Glen Byam Shaw who doubled the Prince and the Cripple and who would become a firm friend.

The Miracle ran on for about four months. Mrs Earle who was cooking for some people in a flat near Baker Street, told me of a room, newly decorated and unfurnished, that was going for a pound a week at the top of a house opposite. It was practical to get the rest of our furniture out of store and use this as a London base; after her other work Mrs Earle would slip over the road to look after me. At Chalfont, where I went whenever I could, money was tight; Sean, though he had finished *Within the Gates,* had no plays running, and our sole hope was to accept an offer from Samuel French to buy the amateur rights of *Juno,* the *Plough* and the *Gunman* for three hundred pounds and a perpetual half-share of royalties. It meant for both of us a long spell of fidgety labour, writing the stage directions in that tiresome shorthand and adding essential diagrams. As G.B.S. said, the sale was a bad mistake, but we had to do it, for Sean was proud about borrowing and the few friends we approached had said that at the moment their money was tied up.

We had to be thinking of a nursery school for Breon. I felt I ought to bring him up as a Catholic, an extravagant wish apparently, for the nuns I saw at a convent in Gerrards Cross asked absurd fees and would not budge. In the end we sent him to a little Quaker school at Jordans which he loved. This was a mercy – one of the few. Chalfont for us was the unhappiest period in our marriage. While I was working, Sean had no companions except a lay brother from Gerrards Cross, the chatty 'Father Clematis', an Irishman who gratefully escaped from the district; and the bachelor owner of a modern laundry who, long ago, had been a violinist in the St James's Theatre orchestra. He lived with an old housekeeper and Sean might have tea there once a week. Not a riotous life: the Chalfont atmosphere would have been deadly to any Irishman, let alone Sean. When you walked through the village the people peered at you over their gates, barely giving you the time of day. We might have been freaks, and doubtless in Chalfont we were an odd couple: Sean much older than me and a trifle grim some-times, whereas I looked about cheerfully at everything and everybody, hoping that one of the gate-gazers might talk. (They never did.) Chalfont life struck me as being on the savage side. Geese hissed and strutted. In the centre of it all a village idiot sat, appropriately, on the village green; I was scared of both idiot and geese. Away on the other side of the main road, City men had their modern bungalows and houses in fairly large gar-dens: the centre of a competitive outer-suburban life with a 'two-car bracket' as the highest ambition, one car for a husband to drive to town and a smaller run-about for his wife. Having no car, we were on the bread-line. It was the silliest move we had made; town people at heart, both of us, we ought to have rented a cheaper London flat. But one cannot live one's life backwards.

I did suggest to my mother that she came to stay with us for a while, a doomed idea from the start. Living in the deep country which she hated, she could not go out even for a drink. The atmosphere grew so tense that she had to leave. Though she loved Breon, she insisted on continually washing his hands and face, and no one who does that to a small boy is noticeably popular.

E

IV

Arthur Sinclair, who was managing the Irish Players, had no work for himself or the company. Hopefully, he asked if Sean could write any sketches for them to do on the music-halls, and Sean, glad to get away from what he called 'the belly of Bucks', replied with *The End of the Beginning*, a kitchen-comedy from an old folk-tale, and the farce of *A Pound on Demand*. Sinclair failed to get them on. When Macmillan published them during 1934 in *Windfalls*, a collection of stories, plays, and poems, Sean said in his preface: 'No attempt was made to market them, and they shiver among the unemployed.' That is no longer true. They are very funny in text and performance, especially *A Pound on Demand* where the monarch of all drunks, nursed by his friend, cannot even write his signature on a Post Office withdrawal form:

> JERRY: Now you've only just to gather the pen into your mitt 'n slap down the old name on the form . . . Try to keep a grip on it, man, 'n don't be spillin' it all over the place. (SAMMY *grips it like a sword*) Aw, not that way. Don't go to the opposite extreme. (*Arranging pen*) Nice 'n lightly between the finger 'n thumb. That way, see? . . . He's not used to this kind of thing, miss, but he'll be all right in a minute.
>
> SAMMY (*standing still and looking vacantly at the wall*): Wanna poun' on demand.
>
> JERRY (*encouragingly*): Go on, bend your back 'n write your name. (*To a* WOMAN *who is writing a letter*) Mind movin' over as far as you can, ma'am, to give him room to write his name – he wants a pound on demand . . .
>
> WOMAN (*indignantly*): This is a nice way to be scattered about, writing an important letter to Tarraringapatam!

Sean had been battling with the Inland Revenue. In a first stage direction he lists, among notices that should hang in the Post

Office: 'Cardinal Virtues: Temperance, Prudence, Fortitude,
Payment of Income Tax.' It sounds like an O'Casey family
motto.

Four months after *The Miracle* Cochran sent for me again,
now for *Mother of Pearl*, a musical with a libretto by A. P.
Herbert and the warm-hearted Alice Delysia as leading lady: she
was 'La Pavane' who has had many lovers and who sings 'Every
woman thinks she wants to wander.' I had a small part and
understudied the inevitable French maid who was called Fifi
this time. Rehearsing late in 1932, we opened with a few Christmas holiday weeks in Manchester, which I loathed, though I do
recall walking round with Alan Herbert, tall, exuberant, and
energetic, with a highly personal sense of humour; he bought
some of his books and signed them for me. I was beginning to
get dissatisfied with being absent so much from Sean and Breon,
and even now I regret having been away from home when Breon
had a really bad bronchial attack.

In London, at the old Gaiety Theatre in the Strand, we had
what was known as a mild Press, the overture to a moderate
run, no more. I did play Fifi several times when Eve Manning
was off, but this pulling against my marriage and struggling
with my ambition had begun to wear me down. It seemed futile.
I had married a man who should have had me with him constantly, and when the show ended its six months I was over-
joyed to be back. For the next months, calmly and dully, I
slipped into the Chalfont domestic routine.

Sean's health was poor. He grew so unwell, indeed, that we
had to take advice in London. At one point we persuaded ourselves dramatically that he would have heart trouble for the
rest of his life, and it was something of an anti-climax when
Dr Bertram Nisse told him that he had merely upset his system
by chain-smoking and must give it up. Both of us were relieved
to have other news. Norman Macdermott, tenant of the Royalty
in Dean Street, Soho – the theatre where Fagan put on *Juno*
in 1925 – offered now to stage *Within the Gates*. Eugene O'Neill
had praised its 'rare and sensitive poetic beauty'; the chance

was overdue; and Macdermott proposed an advance payment
that we needed urgently even if it had to be shared with the
musician Herbert Hughes. He had adapted or composed the
simple tunes Sean had specified for such lines as the *Spring
Chorus*:

> Our mother, the earth, is a maiden again, young, fair, and a
> maiden again.
> Her thoughts are a dance as she seeks out her Bridegroom,
> the Sun, through the lovely confusion of singing of birds,
> and of blossom and bud.

While we were puzzling where to stay in London during rehearsals, Lady Astor invited us to St James's Square: we had her
daughter's charming flat, a bed-sitting-room and the bathroom
of my dreams, at the top of the house. Sean, who had met her
often with G.B.S., knew Nancy better than I did: totally opposed in politics, they respected each other as people. She could
be frightening, but she never bothered me for a moment; I
appreciated her brusque, direct manner as much as her hospi-
tality. It soothed us both to get back to St James's Square from
some depressing days at the theatre where many backers unknown to us seemed to hold a long, gay party; you heard little
serious talk in an upper office among the sherry-drinkers and
the cries of 'Hello, darling!' While so testing a play was
being rehearsed there might have been a testing discussion.

Within the Gates began in February 1934. It had fine
moments, I thought, even if it failed to come across as a whole
in a production that disappointed Sean. Macdermott could be
an able director; his wife designed skilfully the gauze curtain
of the Park gates, 'stiff and formal, dignified and insolent',
which opened, as Sean wished, at the beginning of each scene
and shut at the close. Our friends rallied for the première, the
Shaws, the Cochrans, Lady Astor, Lady Londonderry and Lady
Rhondda (for whom Sean wrote in the weekly *Time and Tide*),
but in under a month the play was off, a sad fate after all Sean's
work. Still, he did have some luck when an American director

went to the Royalty and promised him a production on Broadway.

V

Life at Chalfont could not drift on for ever. We were well aware of it. I was pregnant again, and we persuaded ourselves that we must return to London. No sooner had we packed up gratefully and unpacked in Overstrand Mansions, Battersea, than Sean had to sail to New York for the American production of *Within the Gates*. It was an awkward moment for us. After money from Macmillan had paid the first quarter's rent, we had next to nothing in actual cash. Sean had his ticket; his expenses were met, and what remained we shared. Leaving with fifteen pounds, he wrote to me later saying he wished to God he had taken the lot: as a first-class passenger he could scarcely scrape up enough for the tips.

When he had sailed I got going again in the usual way, pulling our carpets and curtains to pieces and re-assembling them. That Battersea flat, which faced the Park, never looked right except for the room we used afterwards as a nursery and Sean's own room (where generally we lived), sunny and large and with plenty of space for his books. I had developed a craze for reading. Going round Sean's collection I unearthed Zola, Anatole France, Maupassant and Balzac, reading them all in turn without being able to stop. At last dollars were arriving for me from New York. Enjoying the city and impressed by rehearsals (Lillian Gish excelling as the Young Whore whom Marjorie Mars played in London), Sean also spent hours with his loyal friend and advocate, the critic George Jean Nathan, and even moved into Nathan's hotel. He loved the glitter of New York, its theatres and its skyscrapers; he had the most rewarding company such as Brooks Atkinson, Richard Watts junior and Nathan himself, and he made friends with Eugene O'Neill and Carlotta, Sinclair Lewis and Elmer Rice. As ever he responded to affection and insight. If I had not been having

another child, and he had not wanted to be back with Breon and
me, he might well have stayed there.

Ridiculously, after a New York success that was more artistic
than commercial, *Within the Gates* jolted towards its close
when it was banned in puritanical Boston. Sean was home again
by then, but John Tuerk, the manager, sent him an amusing
letter about an interview with the Mayor of Boston who was
determined there should be no 'dirty plays' in the city:

> . . . As for 'God damn you' that was out of the question, and
> there was no excuse for it. Why not change it to 'God be
> with you'? (I nearly fell under the table at that suggestion),
> and then glowering, he added that he had had lots of com-
> plaints about the play, and he wanted to know what kind of
> a Bishop it was – whether a married Bishop or a Bishop that
> couldn't marry – as if that made any difference to a Bishop
> who had begat a bastard daughter . . . I replied that there was
> no denomination or sect involved as the Bishop was a symbol
> and the play a fantasy . . .

Sean returned burdened with gifts that people had sent to
me, with books for Breon – the first coloured pop-up picture-
books I had seen – and many things for the new baby we were
expecting about Christmas. No one could be certain of the date;
much of the time I spent shuttling between our flat and a
nursing-home, in a fashionable street, that Sean hated at sight.
It was not at all clinical. My room, heavy with Victorian furniture, was very dusty; from the moment he took me, he turned
against it, and in *Time and Tide* he wrote angrily: 'There
seemed to be only one medicine glass, for it was frequently
borrowed for the use of a patient in a bad way with bronchitis.'
Years later he said in *Sunset and Evening Star*:

> Many a time he had sat at Eileen's bedside, fuming at the
> way things were being done . . . fuming so plainly that
> Eileen stretched out a hand to touch his arm, and whispered
> – quiet, Sean, you will only make bad things worse with a

temper. Then he would close his eyes, sever the tension by a
great effort, and sigh for the cowardice of the human
heart . . . The middle class would stick anything to preserve
the wan and wonderful manner of their status, burying
under it the best of their intelligence, energy, and sense.

It was a comfort when Sean visited me by himself; I could
coax him into a good humour. If anyone else happened to be
with me, he sat in glum silence, tutting at the entire place. He
couldn't bear it, it did something to him. Early in January, on
one of our outings from it, we were at a local teashop when I
exclaimed that the baby might come at any moment. Agonising
labour pains began in the very hall of the nursing home and I
was just able to reach my ground-floor room and scramble upon
the bed. We named the boy Niall, and he was born on the day
Within the Gates was banned in Boston.

VI

To help with Breon and Niall I now had Helen, a splendid 19-
year-old country girl, from an institution Violet Melchett had
founded in Chelsea. On one side of it girls were trained to be
nannies in richer families; on the other, where Helen had been,
working-class mothers could leave their children, from baby-
hood, in a day nursery. The boys occupied nearly all my time,
but when Niall was two months old Sean and I did manage to
get a fortnight in Ireland. During this visit we went on business
(about a family legacy) to see my Reynolds aunts in Athlone:
my father's sisters, the elder of them eighty-five, the younger
eighty – still at the farm where my father had lived, still working as they had always done. Sean liked them immediately. It
touched me to know how they had followed my career from
childhood, how proud they had been of my father. I won't say
I was displeased to see on the wall a huge photograph of myself, round-faced, sober, and wearing a medal, which had been

blown up from a postcard sent across when I was thirteen or fourteen and in the convent. Now apparently I had inherited the farm and the money left by my grandfather as he had died intestate and I was the daughter of the eldest son. Aware that the money involved was morally my aunts', I simply put by a certain sum as my mother's share, and left the house and the rest to the old ladies with the aid of a friendly Athlone solicitor.

Back in London we talked about schools with the Shaws at Whitehall Court. G.B.S. held, as I did, that a child must have the right environment and little drudgery. No one at the convent had encouraged us to form personal opinions; if you thought too much for yourself you were in trouble. Doubtless this is why I find it so hard to make a decision and can be led easily to the wrong one. It was a good decision, anyway, to send Breon to a school on the edge of Wimbledon Common that G.B.S. admired. Beltane was a grand relaxed place: its five-to-sevens learned addition and subtraction by 'buying' at a number of tiny shops, and geography by exploring an immense map of one country or another drawn on the classroom floor in bright washable crayon or paint. I found Breon, young as he was, a good companion. On some Sundays we might go early to Billingsgate – I mean early, six or seven o'clock – watch the bustle in the market, the fish being unloaded, the porters with their wooden boat-shaped hats, and then get back to the flat in time for breakfast.

Again I was very close to Sean. He was tired after America; his health worried him; there was so much he wanted to write, and he detested the pot-boiling, his *Time and Tide* articles, a few lectures. Proof-reading strained his eyes, so I would do it with him, soon learning the printers' marks and running quickly through the galleys. We seldom entertained. Odd social occasions irritated him; he preferred to sit with a friend, discussing the subjects that interested them, and I am sure he missed those long conversations in New York. Heaven help me if I had not been able to talk fluently about the shows I had been to, art galleries and pictures, the comedy of life. We talked for hours, but I understood that at a special creative time an artist's work must come first. If I had been dull, he would not have stuck me for a month, let alone a year; and it was his own energetic discussion and his humour that fascinated me.

He was indignant about the British Government's refusal to send back to Dublin the paintings collected by Lady Gregory's nephew, Hugh Lane; he could never enter the room at the Tate without working himself up about the injustice of the thing. We used to go also to the National Gallery and to many smaller exhibitions, though private views – with only a few of us there – might be trying. Once, when I said to him, 'I don't like that, do you?' his answer was so final that I whispered hastily, 'Well, don't say anything, will you? Let's go.' It was too late. The manager bounced up. 'Ah, Mr O'Casey . . . how do you like the paintings?'

A nudge from me. 'All right . . . Some very fine colours. Thank you very much, but we must go now.'

That was not enough. 'Yes,' the man insisted, 'but do tell me in detail what you think.'

My turn, quickly. 'Sean was pleased with the colours. I do hope the artist has a success.' 'But,' said the man, 'Mr O'Casey . . . what do *you* think?'

I was beaten. Sean seemed to rise from his turtle-neck sweater as if coming up for air. 'I think,' he said, 'they are bloody awful!'

When we got outside I had no chance to speak. 'Eileen, I tried to be nice. If the man had let me go and not gone on and on . . . I was lost. I'm sorry.' I knew. Sean, if up against it, could be worse than George Washington.

VII

During the thirties Robert Newton, the actor – and an artist's son – who had opened what used to be the large Grand at

Fulham as a 'Shilling Theatre', put on a revival of *Juno*. No
royalties arrived, and any effort to get them fizzled out. This
coincided with a tax demand. We were frightfully in arrear, and
Sean's accountant advised him to appeal to the Special Tax
Commissioners, an exercise that involved hours and hours of
patient sorting. Those evenings with the bank sheets I dreaded;
everything I had attempted to hide came under the spotlight,
and the bills from Peter Jones in Sloane Square were the worst.
Given the temptation of a running account, I soon lost sight of
the total: when you merely have this or that put down, you
cease to think you are spending, and in no time I would put
down too much. I began to work it off on a method of my own
– pay a little, take a lot – so you can guess why those evenings
before a Grand Reckoning could be murder for me.

They would begin formally with the spreading out of bank
sheets and bills. Next, Sean got clean paper and a pen to list
what we owed. Determined to be tolerant, he would say, 'But,
Eileen, however could you owe so much to Peter Jones?' I would
mumble and stutter, and, if questioned too long, flare up. Upon
which Sean, hoping to calm me, would say, 'Ah, to hell! We'll
pay it when we can,' and it would end in a rally-round, five
pounds to one creditor, ten to the next. Sean would give me a
cheque, for the money (most wisely) was in his own name. Had
it been in mine there would have been nothing for the rally-
round.

When the Commissioners heard Sean's appeal he told them
he had had nothing on for some time and his money had gone
in living expenses. 'And what about the royalties from the
Shilling Theatre?' they asked cunningly. 'Not a penny!' Sean
said, but they disbelieved him. He came home furious and told
me that Bobby Newton was a scoundrel. I tried to persuade him
that Bobby, who had worked with me in *Bitter Sweet*, was
rather a nice man and that maybe he was in money difficulties.
It was not, very likely, a tactful argument.

In later years, during one of our bill evenings in Totnes, Sean,
head in hands, said seriously, 'Mind you, Eileen, it's the simplest

thing in the world to make money. You just have to concentrate.'

'Concentrate?' I said. 'But, Sean, what do you concentrate on?'

'It's no good explaining to you, my dear, you'll never understand. And anyhow you'd never give it full concentration.'

'Well, why in heaven's name don't you concentrate and settle it all?'

'Oh no, Eileen, that would be wasting time. I could do nothing else.'

By now it was like a snatch from one of Sean's comedies. Having agreed that money-making would be easy if only one of us would concentrate on it, the argument ended, as arguments generally did, with a cup of tea.

VIII

At this time we did go fairly often to lunch in Whitehall Court with G.B.S. and Charlotte, and at one of these luncheons G.B.S. was eloquent about a visit to Dartington Hall at Totnes. An exciting school, just the place for the O'Casey children. When Dorothy Elmhirst suggested that we came to see for ourselves, she put up the whole family, Sean, Breon, Niall, Helen, and myself. It was May 1937, a useful means of escape from the Coronation crowds pouring into London; also it was my first visit to Devon, and absorbed by the country and the school, I vowed to get the children there.

Dorothy Elmhirst had spent huge sums on Dartington Hall, modernising it discreetly without spoiling its character. Besides the children's school, which I think had been Leonard Elmhirst's plan and was split between three buildings – nursery, middle, senior, in different areas of the estate – there were other schools for acting, music, and the Jooss Ballet. It was inspiring, and yet I could never be completely relaxed with Dorothy herself. Elegant, charming, she somehow affected me as rich people did when I was a child or a teenager – rather like a cloud descending. If we came to Devon, she said to me during one of our talks, Sean might care to work in the Michael Chekhov theatre at Dartington (Michael was the dramatist's nephew), writing sketches for the students. I told Dorothy it would be better not to ask. Sean was most unlikely to agree, and wouldn't it be a waste of time for a creative dramatist? Clearly ruffled, she remained polite.

In Battersea once more, we began to contemplate a move to Devon, though it would be well over a year before everything was organised. We had a new daily help. Our former one had left us because she was pregnant and about to be married. So I called at the local agency and presently Ruth appeared, an elderly woman weighed down by references from the best families. When I said that our small job and ordinary life might not suit her, she answered that now she was older she could no longer stay in 'good service'. That put me in my place, but she was so eager that I said yes.

'Mind you, madam,' she warned me, 'I cannot work too hard. If I do I shall swell up.'

'Oh!' I said. 'Well . . . I don't think there's much hard work here. But, honestly, in the circumstances, perhaps I'd better not have you.'

She drew herself up. 'I am going to work for you,' she said; and the voice reminded me of a dreaded nun in the convent.

'Yes,' I replied meekly. 'Can you start tomorrow?'

Tomorrow Ruth started, at ten o'clock. I was up and dressed. Helen had pushed Niall out in his pram and disappeared to Battersea Park. Breon had gone to school. Sean, racing through breakfast, shut himself into his room, telling me there was no need to touch it. On Ruth's arrival it was plain that she was a lonely person who lived in the past and needed her fanciful kind of existence. I tried to get her to work in either the morning or the afternoon; but as an old-fashioned maid she had morning and afternoon uniforms, and she loved to wear them both. So she would come at eleven in a blue cotton dress and an apron, get our lunch, tidy the flat, and stay for tea. Breon was at school until four-thirty. I let her use his little room to rest and change, and about three o'clock she emerged in a black dress with a smart apron and a cap. It was a pity we had few callers to see her full uniform. Helpfully, I might invite to tea Mrs Hardman Earle (Maie Drage) and her small son, or Helen Elliott, or other friends. Our Helen Hoover was ready to ask other nannies and their charges and Ruth would be coaxed to join them after laying a beautiful nursery tea.

She liked to tell stories of her 'better service', rarely with masters or mistresses, mostly with His Lordship or Her Ladyship. Though they frequented the grandest functions, very often on the night before they had to get their diamonds out of pawn or from the bank. Everyone Ruth had worked for seemed to have been vaguely immoral – her stories reminded me of 'What the Butler Saw' in the seaside peepshows. Indeed she never seemed to come across a moral person in the whole of the 'better service' she so vastly enjoyed.

True, I am not sure of the grand lady who put on a form of rubber bathing suit and ran twice round the Serpentine every morning. It was Ruth's job to see her out of the door and back again, extricate her from the rubber get-up, watch her into a hot bath, and massage her.

'Did she lose a lot of weight?' I asked anxiously.

'Well, madam, she just lost what she put on each day.'

Ruth was on top of her form when she answered the telephone. She would say 'Madam is out,' or whatever it might be; but if anyone inquired for Sean, she would answer sternly, 'I am not allowed to disturb the master.' Our friends always rang back to ask what in heaven had happened. When I did have people to tea, Ruth never felt the table looked up to much and she would bring in her own silver cake-stand. One guest said while Ruth was still in the room, 'Wherever did you get that damn thing from, Eileen?' and I had to shoot out a kick under the table.

Happily, though she might have had a ghost or two in better

service, Ruth never noticed the strange atmosphere – creepy if you let it prey on you – somewhere at the back of our flat. No trouble in Breon's tiny room where he would play quietly, or do puzzles on the hinged window-shelf I made for him. But my own room was dark and congested, with a strange aura, and we believed definitely that the bathroom was haunted. Sean occasionally would be quite faint; I never was, though my imagination made me hurry in and out. Why, when I had a comfortable bathroom at last, must the damn place be haunted as well?

It would not baffle us much longer. Crazily – for the notion was far beyond our means – we decided to send the boys to Dartington as day pupils. Disapproving of boarding-schools as we did, the only plan was to live in Devon ourselves. The agents consented, so we thought, to take over the remainder of our Battersea lease which had approximately a year to run; Sean, Niall, Breon and Helen travelled to Totnes; and I stayed to arrange the storage of our furniture at Harrods (an in-and-out club for us) until we had a place to live. At heart I was dubious about leaving London again so relatively soon. But the move probably would be wise; I guessed, too, that country life would be cheaper, and a phrase of Shaw's kept recurring: 'It will all be managed somehow.' In two words, that was how the O'Casey life was managed then – just somehow.

CHAPTER TWELVE

A House in Devon

WE were not staying in the Hall this time but in the lodge at the drive gates, where the gardener's Welsh wife could not have been kinder. Sean had made progress with a new play, *The Star Turns Red*; strongly dramatic, it symbolised the war of Communism against Fascism. 'Like a good Protestant,' G.B.S. would say of this, 'you have brought the language of the Authorised Version back to life.' He was thinking also of a 'wayward comedy' about a pair of English plutocrats who search for Irish country life in the shell of a Tudor mansion falling to 'purple dust and murmuring ashes'. Frequently misunderstood, this is, in his own words, a tale of 'those who clutch at things that are departing and try to hold them back. So do Stoke and Poges, digging up old bones and trying to glue them together again. They try to shelter from the winds of change, but Time wears away the roof, and Time's river eventually sweeps the purple dust away.' Besides these, and a second Dublin volume of autobiography, he was toiling at occasional articles; he could never work at speed as some journalists do.

Even with the light on, the lodge's sitting-room was very dark, and by the time we moved, in the early autumn of 1938, the light was going at five o'clock. Sean was incapable of working earlier in the day – perhaps an article, but no imaginative writing. Even reading in the poor light was a labour, though not what it had been in the Chalfont cottage. At Dartington he could sit at a table with the light falling on his typewriter and somehow prod and peer along.

Once I had joined him at Dartington he was happier. Every

day we hunted for a house; fewer to let than we had imagined. At length, on the main road in the heart of Totnes itself, we discovered Tingrith, Victorian and ugly, a marvellous place for a family and at a low rent. Its outbuildings had been stables; it had a garage, a conservatory, a bit of front lawn, and at the back a nice rough orchard with plum and apple trees. Tingrith was rather dilapidated, and it had a lot of that brownish, near-cream paint common in so many Victorian houses. But I was excited over it all; a new house and a sense of adventure in a strange land.

So yet again we sent for our furniture – it could almost have found us on its own. Sean's room to begin with: I knew the rules by now, but he stood round under our feet, waiting to be installed. Daily we heard his plaintive murmur, 'Surely to God it doesn't take that long to get one room ready?' It was a big one with wide windows, though greenery was already encroaching on them and the light would suffer. Soon, in spite of the books piled and scattered across the floor, Sean's divan was up, his table, desk and armchair were in place, and his fire was crackling. That evening he disappeared behind a firmly shut door: his home, his room. He sat in his armchair with a sigh of relief. When I glanced in he was almost caressing his typewriter; he might well have been on that letter to a friend in Dublin in which he said (October 1938):

What a time of chassis! Putting everything back in another place, and finding the place the wrong one. And the whole place gutted with dugouts, caverns, pits, trenches, with gasmen and electric men yelling havoc all the time. When most of the devastation was over, it was found out the gasmen had put their pipes too near the electric cable, and so all had to be done again . . . The country feels very curious after London. The change is a gamble, and we must abide by the hazard of the die.

As soon as our beds were up, we struggled on. Painting next: I had to get rid of that brown underground-lavatory colour. The

poor old carpets we had splashed our money on in St John's Wood had been twice cut to size, at Chalfont and Battersea; now at Tingrith we made them over for the last time. One square went to the large front room where the surround had to be varnished. Other fragments we cut up for the front stairs, and elsewhere we had to do with rather shiny second-rate linoleum and a few rugs.

In the middle of the fun I heard from Ruth. She was coaxing me to let her come down if only for a few weeks – 'to help you settle'. Some people affect me like this; I can't say no, and I couldn't here. Sean and Helen considered tactfully that it might be useful for Ruth to cook our meals while we put Tingrith in shape; and she duly arrived to find us in a house with front and back stairs, a refinement that greatly impressed her. Since the task for her declining years was to see that the O'Caseys lived like ladies and gentlemen, she set out again to be a real maid to us: blue cotton uniform in the morning, black-and-white with cap at four in the afternoon. Alas, almost as in Battersea, no one saw the cap but some stray people who dropped in to ask if they could do anything. Ruth fought on. At first she got breakfast: pure agony because Helen and I had usually rushed everything on the table and hurried Breon off to school and Niall to his nursery class. Sean never appeared until much later. When Ruth took over we had to have the table laid properly as in the Better Service. It took hours while we sat waiting for breakfast or toast, trying not to offend her or to send the children off starving. After two days I couldn't bear it. I told her to get up when the children had gone and to lay breakfast simply for myself and Sean, 'the master'. The thing grew ludicrous. Right after breakfast she brushed the front stairs; properly (her favourite word) it should have been done before breakfast, though what was the good of that when we had to plod up and down for our painting, I never could fathom.

There had to be a climax. Hurrying in one afternoon with three or four children from school, Breon demanded egg and chips. Ruth had laid the tea with cake, bread and butter and jam, but I pulled myself together and said, 'Ruth, can you possibly do some egg and chips?' She said in italics: *'Egg and chips!* At this hour of the day? It isn't *done!'* 'Oh, come on, Ruth!' I exclaimed; at which, going red, she went upstairs with dignity, a rebellious cap and apron. I did the egg and chips myself.

That evening I said as kindly as I could, 'Ruth, you are wasting your good service on us. We lead a very ordinary life; you'll be most unhappy, and I cannot even afford you. Why don't you just stay for a week on holiday and go off every morning to see the beauties of Devon? But by bus – we haven't a car.' By the end of the week she had realised that the O'Caseys would never be ladies and gentlemen, and fondly she said goodbye. All this because I had lacked courage enough to say no in the beginning.

II

One of our Tingrith headaches was how to keep the place warm. We had excellent grates, and Sean longed passionately to have a cellar full of coal. It would hold a lot and he never economised, a throw-back to Dublin days, I suppose, when the fire was the spirit of his room and he even cooked on it. Three boards, fitting into slots, divided the Tingrith cellar. When the three were set, the cellar was full; it grew emptier as each board was removed, but – however hard up we were – we never got to the third. (In any event, Totnes tradespeople were most trusting.) Sean liked to fill the buckets himself, the work of a few hours; he had a large kitchen range going, a fire in his own room and one upstairs in a playroom-nursery. With coal so expensive we got plenty of logs from the Dartington Hall sawmills, and even then Sean felt the cold appallingly. We had to use oil-stoves on the landing by the lavatory, and in an enormous bathroom (another for my collection) where our landlord, a dentist, had established his surgery and pulled out the teeth: we kept a stove there for at least an hour before anyone could have a bath.

Obviously, we missed Billy McElroy's hand in the coal-cellar. That friendship had waned since Chalfont because of Sean's response (or lack of it) to the current lady-love. A married man and many years older than she was, Billy expected us all to share his infatuation. About thirty, rather demure and quite pleasant-looking, she was divorced with two small children. Sean and I thought little of her, but at Chalfont Billy would make her walk in front of us as if she were a model. 'You don't mind, Kathleen dear?' he would say, 'We want to admire your legs.' This was idiotic. However he admired the girl – who left him in the end for another business man – we were in no mood for swooning; Sean, being Sean, was deeply bored. Then political views began to clash, and Billy faded out of our lives.

We went on knowing his son Con, who often came to see us and talked of his father, a lovable rogue if the roguery did not harm you. Like so many business men, Billy – in spite of a very generous streak – dwelt perpetually on money-making. I agree that without money we cannot express our personalities or live an ordinary comfortable life, but what I dread is the thought of wanting it merely for its own sake.

III

A natural extrovert, I began to pine for London and my friends. At eight o'clock every evening, when the children were in bed and though I might be weary from decorating the house, I was wide awake and ready and eager to go anywhere. Goodness knows where, but the evening for me must be a time for celebration. When people tell me how they love to be alone, I just envy them and feel a little disbelieving. At Tingrith now I had to sit until ten when Sean, who had dug into his work immediately on reaching the house, would stop writing for a bit and discuss it animatedly over his tea.

When actually creating a play he was happy. Early in 1939 I knew I would be having another child, and this delighted us both. Through the spring, and for a month or two in that hot pre-war summer, we lived without incident. Sean, always a townsman, had taken to deep-country Devon much better than I had guessed. It was unlike the Chilterns. Its people (and I am speaking of real Devon farm families) were warm-natured and tolerant, and they would talk to you by the hour even if they might look you over before deciding to be friends. They had no pretensions and they kept their own counsel. Believing in 'little folk' who would come from nowhere to help with the harvest, they even left at night food and cakes that by morning had vanished. One farmer told me seriously that he had been 'pixied' in the middle of a field and that it had taken him hours to get out: no, Mrs O'Casey, not too much cider but the work of a 'bad' pixie who had a grudge against him and in revenge had blighted the harvest.

Totnes was charming: a hilly main street with an ancient castle above it; a market-place, off the centre, for chickens, eggs, and butter; at the top of the town, a cattle market; and, behind the High Street, some fine old houses. Often, where shop-keepers lived above their shops, there were Adam ceilings and mantelpieces. The rest of the town was divided by class. We lived ourselves in the middle-class region with a bank manager on our right and the manager of Buckfastleigh woollen mills on the left. Elsewhere there were rows and rows of council houses and the smart Bridgetown district, where I knew only one person, our Dr Varian, a Dubliner, who was a great friend.

Sean described Totnes in a *West Country Magazine* article, only once, I think, reprinted in full, though he quoted some of it in the last volume of his autobiography:

This Devon town is as old as the hills around it, or as the river Dart that wanders by, with the town's feet almost dangling in its quiet waters. Here from a golden-sailed galley, with a silver prow and a bronze helm, shortly after the world began there landed a Trojan Chief who had married the King of Greece's daughter. Both of them had fled hot-foot

through the flaming fires of Troy (Totnes's first evacuees) to settle down, and rear a family whose descendants gave to the country some of those warriors who did their share in holding up England for the world to see. There, to this very day, in the prime street of the town, is the stone where the feet of Brutus first landed when he took a flying leap to the shore from the galley to abide in Devon with the Briton forever.

And again (he was writing just after the war):

The market-place is still a weekly blossom of the town, but its petals are no longer of a rich texture, and the colours are gone. Now it seems to be but a collection of a few green leaves and a handful of berries. God be with the time when the place was giddy with profusion. How often have my wife and I gone home from the market gaily burdened with goods; heavy-laden with butter with a favourite taste from a farm that we almost looked upon as our own; with thick cream, fruit still adorned with the velvety bloom of Eden; more eggs than we knew what to do with; under her arm, a chicken; under mine, a duck; and the generous Devon dialect, alert and luminous, serious and merry, around us.

This is good to remember, but our first Devon summer was darkened. Nothing to do with Totnes. Six months after we had left Overstrand Mansions, the agents, who had apparently freed us from the rest of our lease, now demanded a year's rent. They could do it because it was not confirmed in writing that our lease had ended. We fought the case strongly. At midsummer we went to London and gave evidence at the Law Courts, an exhausting business, for I was well on in my pregnancy. The final judgement was against us. Morally we were justified, legally not ('good law and poor equity' said Sean), and it cost us about £300. We were still trying to recover from this when the declaration of war on that Sunday in September changed our lives in Totnes as all over Britain. I stopped concentrating on myself

and the child and ceased to be lonely or to fret for London. Now
one had to be thinking of the rest of the world.

IV

We were among the first provincial towns to get evacuees. They
poured into Totnes Station by the trainload, clutching their little
bundles and with tickets round their necks; and until they
could be sorted out and sent to various local families, they
huddled by the hundred in the big Jooss Ballet School which
Dartington Hall had thrown open. Though we all tried to make
as much of a party of it as we could, many of the poor children,
the smaller ones particularly, were bewildered and pathetically
lost. At Tingrith we took on three ourselves, a girl of about
twelve, another of five and a boy of three, from the inner East
End: all in a dreadful state, lice-ridden and never house-trained.
They were not miserable, which was something; they had kept
together, and the eldest, Doris, who was about twelve and ille-
gitimate, behaved like a mother to Zoë and Bobby, the younger
ones, aged five and three. Joy, a local girl who had been helping
at Tingrith in the mornings, now stayed on for most of the
day. Totnes working-class families were generally clean and
well cared for; Joy would never have met anything like this,
and the children's condition appalled her – I can see her ex-
pression yet as she opened the strong-smelling bundles, grey
with dirt, and plunged them into a tub of soapy water while
we rustled up clothes for the children to wear. Helen had known
plenty of dirt and poverty when she worked at the Melchett
day nursery, and Sean, who could recall the slums of Dublin –
and was indeed writing of them at the time – was not as shocked
as I was. As young children at the orphanage we had been kept
spotless, and these sights were entirely strange to me. Sean
wrote to George Jean Nathan:

Better send you a greeting before the going gets too bad.
Here we are in the midst of darkness; every window blinded

and the right hand on a gas mask. We have three poor kids from London stopping with us; these, with our own two, and one more coming, makes things lively. I have to give a hand with the making of the beds, etc. A good job I've been used to kids from my youth up. Concerning the theatre, O'Casey's occupation's gone. I'll have to try to look around for some other things to write about to keep the kettle on the hob . . . We are all well, though Eileen is feeling the job of bearing a baby a bit.

Before the baby arrived I had to stay in Torquay for about a fortnight to have a series of injections at Torbay Hospital. We had begun the blackout. Niall, Breon and the evacuees I left with Helen and Joy. But then my mother, who had stayed all this time in London (and I was not sorry) turned up in Devon; while ill in hospital she had got them to send her for convalescence to a home in Torquay.

On the morning we met I was as enormous as I always was when pregnant, wearing a kind of tent-coat, but facially (again as usual at these times) looking rather good, my hair well brushed and neat. We met outside Torquay's main store. I kissed her. She kissed me. Then she spoke.

'You look absolutely frightful. What have you got on?'

'Oh, don't worry,' I said, 'I'm enormous, but I feel fine. Don't you think I look well?'

'My dear child, I never thought to see you like this.'

Of course. It dawned on me that for years she had known me in London, dressed up. Here in the country I had sandals and no stockings, brown legs (it was the end of the summer), and hair tied back from my face in a band. To her I was a gipsy. We went for lunch to a smart teashop where people said, 'Hello, Eileen!' or 'How well you look!' which cheered me a bit; but when we parted she was telling me with relish that I was in for a terrible time. I had been feeling on top of the world; now I was down, dull, and heavy. More trouble, I thought. She would have to be disposed of somewhere.

Shivaun, a lovely, black-curled baby, was born in Torbay Hospital on an evening of late September. The Scottish doctor, who had been on good terms with Sean during my pregnancy, was proud of her; so were the nurses who carried her through the wards to show her off. I was so happy to have a girl. Before long I could leave hospital and return with her to Tingrith where Breon and Niall, with the evacuee children cleaned up, were waiting for us at a festival tea.

As we pierced deeper into the war, life expanded in a strange and furious rush. Sean put it like this in *Sunset and Evening Star*:

Eileen was never so busy. Minding the latest infant, she forced time to let her gain a first-class certificate in the science of first-aid; she practised how to deal with an incendiary bomb, creeping, done out in dungarees, on her belly into a hut filled with old furniture, set ablaze with magnesium. Within smoke and fume and heat of the blaze she worked the hose of a stirrup-pump . . . till the flames died, and curling smoke round the charred furniture showed that danger was over.

Then, each day, she hurried up to Dartington to help with the midday meal for the refugee children, watching warily and brightly over her own flock in her spare time; for she and he often spent anxious times till their two lads were safely home from school, having passed through the sullen black-out of the bitter wintry evening. So many women had been called to the colours that housewives with children had now more work than three of them would be expected to do normally.

This was the period when the Home Guard was formed, in Totnes a splendid, patriotic lot who, when drilling in various shapes and sizes, could really look rather comic. On Sundays, for their regular exercising, one route to a large field near us was up our drive, through the back garden, and over the roof of the outside lavatory. Some were hard put to it to walk

quickly, much less to run, and it delighted us to see them push-
ing each other over the lavatory roof. Goodness knows who or
what they were going to save during these exercises – every
Sunday we seemed to be watching a brisk music-hall turn.

V

When Sean developed bronchitis our evacuees became more than
we could cope with; they left us for a good working-class family
in the district, though they often came back to see how we
were. Later, in 1941, I had the most strenuous job of all,
running a shop as local organiser of the Mrs Churchill Aid to
Russia Fund, arranging concerts, dances, whist drives, and
getting people to give us such things as children's clothes, which
were suddenly very scarce.

Before this there had been our heaviest air raids. We had to
watch the blackout carefully because Totnes was on almost a
direct route to Plymouth. The great western city was attacked
fiercely and regularly in the spring of 1941, and even now it is
eerie to re-live those nights governed by the howl of the sirens,
often two or three consecutive warnings. The all-clear would
go; maybe half an hour afterwards we were dragged from bed
again, back and forth, back and forth, a thoroughly tiresome
business. Originally an adventure for the children, we sheltered
in the cellar, getting down to it by a ladder from the kitchen.
We had made it as habitable as we could by painting boxes and
slinging hammocks, but it was a damp, smelly hole and we felt
that very likely the entire house would fall in on us. Instead
we adjourned to the Anderson shelter, a form of steel cage
established in a little spare room by the hall door. Shivaun, a
baby when it all started, enjoyed being roused in the middle of
the night and nothing frightened her. The rest of us sat listening to the throbbing of distant aircraft and the distant crashes.
When chased, the Germans had a knack of dropping their
bombs anywhere to lighten the load, and we could never be

sure. Fortunately, most of the bombs fell on fields outside the town.

Breon, at thirteen or fourteen, was the only one of us who could sleep soundly through the lot, except when a louder crash suggested that raiders were getting close – then he would take the stairs at a bound. On the worst nights he was good at cheering Niall, always nervous and looking as if he might faint; Breon's chatter would make him forget. Much to me is still unforgettable: the moments after a raid, for example, when you peered through the blackout and saw the far sky in a blaze of red from burning Plymouth. It seemed frightful that such beauty could derive from such havoc.

Sights could be grim by day. During one of the quick, pouncing raids we got sometimes, two young soldiers were standing on Totnes Station at the end of a leave, waiting to catch a train back to their unit. A first bomb struck the railway bridge, a second the platform – and, by the terrible irony of war, the boys who had come through so far without a scratch were killed instantly. I think, too, of the beautiful sunny afternoon when a direct hit killed nearly every child at Sunday school in a Torquay church. Their parents were inconsolable. 'She didn't want to go,' one said to me. 'I merely sent her out so that I could get a few hours' peace. How was I to know?' These now are the things one remembers.

It worried Sean when any of us went to Torquay for shopping or the odd film, though he understood that sometimes we must run the risk. With a friend I took Niall in to a children's film; afterwards I was in a panic at the bus stop, aware how alarmed Sean would be if he woke and could not find us. The first bus was overloaded. I begged the conductor, a man I knew, to let Niall and myself get on it (our friend could have followed later), but it was impossible; we had to wait for another long twenty minutes. And then it occurred to me that we were on an unusual route to Totnes; still, some of the buses had to serve different villages, and in any event we did get home about five. On the news that evening we heard that the bus we were to

have caught had been hit by a bomb, many passengers killed, and most of the remainder injured.

VI

I had never wanted to drive a car in the days when Helen Elliott was urging me to learn and my boy-friends could have taught me. But just before the war I changed my mind; it did seem my one hope of freedom to get round outside Totnes, and I bought a battered little Morris, not simply old but ancient. It never liked to start; one had to shake it vigorously to operate whatever had failed to click. The patched-up radiator was always leaking, and in an emergency we stuck chewing-gum over the leak until we could get to a garage. Once the steering-wheel came off in my hand; I just contrived to glide into a hedge.

Nobody could have had L plates longer than I did, but I told myself it ought to make other people take care. My teacher, the garage-man, agreed that my steering was a bit individual – I had never even ridden a bicycle – but he was amiable enough to say on taking me down a quiet lane to practise, 'Well, Mrs O'Casey, I did have one lady worse than you . . . I had to take her into a field for a week to get her to steer straight.' Cows scared me. Out by myself, and driving tentatively through a lane, I ran into an entire herd, lost what nerve I had, and barged into the middle of them. Whereupon one promptly sat on the bonnet and decorated it. What's more, the heavy cow did no good to a tinny car. With a dented wing I returned to my garage where they uncreased the dent and washed the bonnet. Sean, when I told him, said loyally, 'I'm certain, dear, it wasn't your fault. It must have been the cow's.'

I did get my provisional licence, and during the war I was allowed to use the car for certain purposes. Sean had to be driven to and from Plymouth for eye treatment, and he had to go frequently to an ear specialist in Torquay. Sometimes I brought the children back from school. I had begun to drive fairly well, even if the children wondered whether I might stall the car or shove my foot on reverse and go backward. It was wise to have persevered: the car was a blessing, and I even managed to drive in the blackout, although, hating it as I did, I developed a habit of losing my way on roundabouts and going many miles in the opposite direction.

VII

When America entered the war every G.I. must have descended on Totnes overnight. Tents blossomed in the local park, on the banks of the river, and up the drive to Dartington Hall estate; officers were billeted in a number of the estate houses and in buildings that had been commandeered for them. By our standards the Americans were rich and spent freely – exciting for Totnes girls and hard on our own soldiers who had nothing like the same means. Lonely soldiers, drunk every night on Devon cider, talked their hearts out to us. Coloured men, late-comers, were the loneliest of all. At a picnic with Shivaun and some other children on the river bank, I sat by a wistful G.I. from Alabama, who proved to be a camp cook; he was so happy to be with a family for a few hours, and I thought how nonsensical it was that he should have been brought over to fight in a war he knew nothing about – I hope he saw Alabama again. Sometimes at night, in and out of a town pub, a private war would start up – almost to bloodshed – between white and coloured soldiers, men taken from their homes to fight in the same cause and now, after too much Devon cider, trying to kill each other over a trivial difference.

I am not harping upon this, for most of the Americans we met were delightful and Sean gained by their coming. Many more visitors he enjoyed talking with arrived at Tingrith, some, particularly, who were not stationed in Totnes. Thus Tom (Thomas Quinn) Curtiss, a New York drama critic, who had turned sergeant in the Intelligence Service and worked at Allied Headquarters in London, travelled down to us with a letter from Nathan. He and Sean sat far into the evening, and he spent the night with a typescript of *Oak Leaves and Lavender*. Dave Greene, a University teacher in civilian life, would rattle up with a friend in their jeep from billets near Plymouth. Students among ordinary G.I.s in Totnes would call on us: Tingrith now seldom had a quiet night.

Sean at this time was well into a third book of autobiography, *Drums Under the Windows*. He had published the second part, *Pictures in the Hallway*, and the text of his play, *Red Roses For Me* (he thought originally of calling it *Asea in a Gold Canoe*), with its famous description, 'A gold-speckled candle, white as snow, was Dublin once; yellowish now, leanin' sideways, and guttherin' down to a last shaky glimmer in the wind of life.' Much of Sean himself is in the idealistic Ayamonn, Protestant in love with a Catholic, who sees the shape of a new world in the shilling a week for which the railwaymen are striking; and Sean's own mother Susan could have partly suggested Ayamonn's mother with the plants in her tenement room:

> Under the window, on a roughly made bench, stand three biscuit tins. In the first grows a geranium, in the second, musk, and in the third, a fuchsia. The disks of the geranium are extremely large and glowing; the tubular blooms of the golden musk, broad, gay, and rich; and the purple bells of the fuchsia, surrounded by their long white waxy sepals, seem to be as big as arum lilies. These crimson, gold, and purple flowers give a regal tint to the poor rooms.

The transfiguration of listless slum folk on a Liffey bridge, the Bridge of Vision, is also described in *Pictures in the Hallway*: an experience Johnny Cassidy (who is Sean) had as a youth on an evening of late spring at the turn of the century, when he came with his empty handcart to the Liffey quay and saw Dublin glorified in the sunset. In Brennan o' the Moor, 'owner of a few ould houses', Sean remembered a Totnes character he

used to see at the market, and who doubted whether a bank
was really safe enough for his money. 'With cunning confi-
dence,' says Brennan, 'tell me what you think of the Bank of
Ireland.'

Since the war began we had had changes at Tingrith. Helen
had gone to the A.T.S. Joy had married. Shivaun, as she grew
up, kept me busy whatever I was doing (and that was plenty).
Having a raging toothache one day and no one to leave her with
– she was about five – I had to take her with me to Newton
Abbot a few miles away. Niall volunteered to come so that he
could look after her while I was in the dentist's surgery. There
the most sombrely conventional patients sat round the waiting-
room. No one in the heavy silence spoke above a whisper, and
Niall murmured that he might as well take Shivaun to Wool-
worth's where she could buy a present 'to cheer me up'.
Unable to afford it, I hardly drank at all; but now and again,
when thoroughly tired, I did take a gin-and-tonic to the bathroom and have it by me while bathing Shivaun. I expect she
thought it helped me; anyway, as I waited with the rest of the
patients, she danced in, full of excitement, unaware of anybody
else, and handed me a blue plastic mug with a yellow duck on
it.

'Mummy,' she cried, 'for your gin!'

Clearly, I was an alcoholic. The patients stared in horror
as I hugged Shivaun, thanked her very much, and said I was
sure the mug would cheer me up. It did noticeably little to the
other people.

VIII

In May 1945 we heard with uncontrollable emotion that the
war in Europe had ended. That night of early summer everyone, men, women, children, collected torches in the Totnes
market place, carried them to a central spot to be lighted, and
marched in a long column right through and round the town.

An astonishing picture, said Sean, who stood watching at our gate: a quivering blaze that moved slowly uphill while we sang the wartime songs:

She'll be coming round the mountain when she comes . . .
She'll be wearing silk pyjamas when she comes . . .

(I never knew exactly what it meant, but it was a grand marching tune and we sang it lustily); and the American chorus,

This is the Army, Mr Brown,
This is the Army, Mr Green . . .
Please keep the barracks nice and clean . . .

Shivaun, at five-and-a-half, marched with me. Breon and Niall were up at Dartington; as a separate village it celebrated on its own, and into the night we saw the sparkle of its huge bonfire. When Shivaun was asleep I went back to the Totnes Plains where everyone was dancing to music from a loud-speaker, pubs flowed with cider, and the farmers begged you to come in to drink with them. Above, the Dartington bonfire began gradually to smoulder; in the early hours we broke up in ones and twos and made unwillingly for bed.

Next morning was hushed. Could we really have been through it all? Few of us felt we were older, and yet there we were – nearly six years on. In Totnes every hour, every minute of the day, my imagination and energy had been needed and employed: it was years since that anti-climax of the empty evening had troubled me. I was settled into my home and life. Surely, I thought, all gifts and enthusiasms must somehow be employed in a newer world? No; almost within a night the comradeship of the war was over, we slipped back to our respectable dwellings, and where now was the lost Utopia?

CHAPTER THIRTEEN

After the War

WELL, what next? I felt that an elastic band had snapped in my head. In Tingrith and out of it I had been so constantly on the go that I had no idea what to make of a lull in which nothing happened and for which we were unprepared. Certainly I was: the friendliness of our Totnes fraternity seemed to have vanished in a few hours. But though Sean's work had been interrupted, he had published a good deal and written more. He was submerged now in *Inishfallen, Fare Thee Well*, the fourth volume of his autobiography. The third, *Drums Under the Windows*, was written, and due that year; and the fantasy of *Oak Leaves and Lavender*, the play Tom Curtiss had read through the night on his first visit, was waiting for a manager.

I missed the hundred obligations of the war period, but domestically one could hardly be idle; Tingrith hummed with all the problems inseparable from an old Victorian house in the 1940s. One tiny thing. As it was impossible to meet the bills ('economic dislocation' was Sean's phrase) we had to do our laundry at home and buy a cheap washing machine: among the O'Caseys an event. The wringer had to be turned by hand. At first Shivaun and Niall were eager to help, but this eagerness could hardly last. Niall, now in the Dartington senior school, was a person apart. He tore round as much as the others, but he never looked untidy. Football shirt and cricket flannels had to be spotless, and it was an effort to remove the grass stains from the knees of his white trousers. With Shivaun to

look after when she got in from nursery school, I had enough
on my hands; yet in the evenings, and dangerously, that old
pre-war restlessness returned.

We entertained very little. During our fifteen-odd years at
Totnes the Elmhirsts dined with us just once; the military
historian Basil Liddell Hart and his wife, who lived in a house
opposite, came once or twice; and so did Bill Curry, headmaster
of Dartington, and his wife Marsie. Inexplicably, I was far too
nervous. Rarely, we went up to the Elmhirsts'; Sean, after dinner one night, read passages from *Finnegans Wake*, explaining
to some of Dorothy's guests how James Joyce had evoked the
city of Dublin. With Dorothy I could not be my natural self.
She cared for the arts, and yet in some ways she overwhelmed
me; again I noticed myself returning subconsciously to those
younger days when richer people patronised me. I was very
friendly with Leonard Elmhirst who sometimes called at Tingrith to chat with Sean. At Christmas, doing the rounds of
various Totnes people connected with Dartington, he would
bring a bottle of wine. A pleasant gesture, for some reason it
infuriated Sean who hated gifts from other than close friends
and believed that Leonard was behaving like a Lord Bountiful
distributing largesse to the tenants.

At Dartington early in 1941 we had real theatre at last:
Basil C. Langton's travelling repertory company which stayed
there for some weeks. Langton could not afford many artists, but
he was a good hand at short-cast plays with such actresses –
young then – as Margaret Leighton and Yvonne Mitchell. Beginning with Coward's *Private Lives*, he went to Patrick
Hamilton's Victorian-period thriller, *Gaslight*, about a suavely
evil husband and terrified wife, and on to Shaw (*Arms and the
Man*), Jean-Jacques Bernard, Emlyn Williams and Priestley.
Splendid, I thought, to have these plays almost at the door, and
at trifling prices: eighteenpence in those days to three-and-six.
Langton would have remained at the Barn Theatre, but strangely
Dorothy would not agree. She came to tea with us to discuss it.
Knowing my enthusiasm, and at the pleading of Basil Langton

F

who called to see him, Sean had written a letter to Dorothy. No use; she would not change her mind, and the company went. Sean wrote to a friend:

A travelling Rep. Co. came here and caught on, but Dartington's Art Dept. has ordered it off, and there's a bit of a rustle going on – perfectly polite and daintily spoken. I have sent in a few sharp comments.

II

Una Albery, who was devoted to Sean, persuaded her husband, the West End manager, Bronson Albery, to stage *Red Roses For Me* in the first months of 1946. He engaged for it a Dublin director, Ria Mooney, who as an actress had been brave enough, when nobody else was, to play the prostitute at the Abbey première of *The Plough and the Stars*. She was strikingly handsome. Sean said of her, 'She's a grand little person,' and Ria said of him, 'I never knew a Sean O'Casey who wasn't kind, gentle, and sensitive.' For all that, nothing would get him to the London rehearsals; it was arranged that I should go instead for the final week and stay for the opening. It seemed to be an age since my last trip. Getting away from Tingrith was a major manœuvre.

Hating me to leave him, Sean would produce a list of questions a mile long. 'What do I do if this or that happens?' he asked, pencil and paper in hand. 'How do I do this, that, or the other?' As if the house were going to collapse round him, he demanded the telephone numbers of all our tradespeople. Then, urgently, 'Don't, for God's sake, let Winnie [our help] in to tidy my room. You can ask her to make the bed, if she likes – not that I can't make my own – if you say she likes doing it . . . She can make up a fire if she likes, but I can make my own fire too . . . You say she'd be awfully upset if she couldn't do it? Oh, well ! . . . when she's done that, tell her not to touch anything on the floor, or on the table, or anywhere else in the room. I think it's an extremely tidy room, there's method in every goddam single piece of paper here! . . . and, by the way, Eileen, tell her not to worry about those ashes round the ashtray because half the time she's tidying these up she has an uncanny habit of losing the very thing I'm working on. And if you're not here to find it, what in the name of God am I supposed to do? . . . Then, dear, she has a habit of cleaning boots that don't need to be cleaned. Tell her not to touch them; in fact, they're too clean . . . Mind you, Eileen, tell her very nicely. I wouldn't like to hurt her, she's a very nice woman.'

I settled Sean, more or less. He had resigned himself to looking after Shivaun; and yet on the night before going away I was in suspense. I could never be quite certain. Creeping to the train next day, I had a vision of Sean calling, or Shivaun running after me; until I actually sat in the compartment with the door slammed and the train in motion, I scarcely drew breath.

Bronson Albery tried out *Red Roses* at the Embassy Theatre, Swiss Cottage: a first night so impressive that I came home excitedly. I was always as full of excitement when returning as when leaving for London. But now Sean and Shivaun, meeting me at Totnes Station, looked miserable; Shivaun was near to tears. 'I'm afraid a very nasty thing has happened,' Sean said, 'poor Kitty has been run over.' Kitty was our cat; that morning she must have had a direct blow from a car – Shivaun had found her at the gate dead but unmarked. 'It's all your fault for going away,' cried Shivaun. 'Kitty was looking for you and couldn't find you.' The only means of cheering her up was to say that Kitty must have a really grand funeral, and next morning this took place in the garden. We put her playthings in the cat's box, made a cross from twigs for the grave, and had an extra-special lunch afterwards, Niall staying home from school for the occasion.

Red Roses came at last to a West End theatre, the New in St Martin's Lane. Here the Alberys became so anxious for Sean to come that he yielded. We both went to London, his first visit in seven years, while Niall boarded at Dartington and Shivaun stayed with her nursery-school teacher. The production pleased Sean, Eddie Byrne's Brennan particularly, and Ria's treatment of the Bridge of Vision where tired Dubliners renewed their youth and vigour in the setting sun: 'There's th' great dome o' th' Four Courts lookin' like a golden rose in a great bronze bowl.'

We lingered for two or three weeks in London so that Sean could consult his eye specialist. It was a depressing report, and his sight had deteriorated so much that he could not move around freely. Though we did some wistful re-visiting, I guessed he was aching to be at home. He grew irritable and impatient. His health was indifferent, and slight silicosis, contracted during his years as a labourer, increasingly affected his chest.

At Tingrith Dr Varian proposed that, as Shivaun now used the spacious, airy playroom much less than she had, Sean should take it over: a sensible plan, for greenery outside the window was darkening the room where he had lived for eight years. To move anyone from downstairs to upstairs sounds nothing. To transfer many hundred books, and to see that the new room is precisely on the pattern of the old, is no joke. We got a two-handled laundry basket, loaded it with books, packed shelf by shelf, and made dozens and dozens of trips, while Sean, in Niall's bedroom opposite, groaned and moaned and asked when in the name of God he could get into his room again. Pottering in and out, he would implore us not to muddle the shelves; in spite of our care, he insisted on stacking the books himself. Winnie and I were practically worn out. She hurried home to get her family's midday meal; and Dr Varian, calling to see how Sean was and discovering me hysterical and in tears, was angry with Sean for the first time since they had met.

'Honestly,' he said, 'it's Eileen who needs a doctor, not you. You must really have some kind of patience while this is going on.'

Patience? Sean was amazed. 'My dear Eileen,' he exclaimed

to me, 'I haven't said a word. I have been sitting here completely quiet. I had no idea I was upsetting anyone – really I *am* sorry.' Winnie came back; Sean rested undisturbed for two or three hours, we finished the books, made up the divan, and settled everything in place. Sean, when he emerged, was solicitous to the last degree.

After those eight years of coal, wood, and tobacco smoke and his horror of dusting anything – for he was convinced that dusting spread germs – the old room looked appalling: quite beyond me to decorate myself, so we employed a professional for the first time. It was turned into a playroom with a litter of children's books and puzzles, and a dressing-up basket for Shivaun and six or seven friends who came in on Saturday mornings to invent plays they would act for us afterwards. Sean, away from everything and everybody, was much snugger upstairs.

III

Youths of eighteen were being called up for two years of military service. In 1946 Breon, who had been about to enter London University, had to leave us: our first family parting, bound to be strange and sad for any mother, and so wasteful when boys straight from school were whipped away from home whether they liked it or not. Luckily, Breon was not going abroad. His first Royal Artillery posting in Taunton was reasonably close; he stayed there for a month and we used to run across and see him.

In the same year Macmillan published Sean's wartime play, *Oak Leaves and Lavender*, originally named *A World on Wallpaper*. This was an allusion to a sentence in Yeats's *Tassie* letter: 'The whole history of the world must be reduced to wallpaper in front of which the characters move and speak.' Mixing fantasy and realism between the shadow-masques of its prologue and epilogue, *Oak Leaves* was set in a Cornish manorhouse during the Battle of Britain. Sean indicated precisely the

various symbolic changes in the staging: 'The columns flank-
ing the doorway have become machinery shafts. The bureau
has become a lathe, though still preserving the vague outline
of what it was once. The two lesser windows have turned into
wheels carrying belts to the chandeliers, now turned up on their
sides and ready to revolve, too, in unison.' It should have been
a test for designer and director; Sean was hopeful when during
1947 Una Albery got her husband to present the play.

Its trial week was at a theatre on the south coast. We went
to Eastbourne, but the rehearsals saddened us: Sean could not
agree with the director who asked for advice and ignored it,
and who neglected the elaborate scenic instructions altogether.
One could either say nothing or have a full set-to. Gallantly,
Sean said nothing. The Eastbourne performances were flat; we
escaped from them to Totnes, but I did go to London in May
for the première at the Lyric, Hammersmith, and Breon got
leave from his unit to be with me. We were glad of that, though
the production deeply embarrassed and disappointed us. I have
never yet seen the play as Sean intended it. Tucked away towards the end of his sixth autobiographical volume, *Sunset and
Evening Star* (1954), you will find his own epitaph on *Oak
Leaves*:

Whenever he ventured to think of what was the worst production of a play of his, his heart's blood pressed into his
head and all the world became red. Even critics, often tolerant of things done badly, declared it to be a butchery of a
play. And one had to bear it quietly, though the heart was
stung. Never before had Sean seen such an assured and mas-
sive incompetency in a producer assigned to the English
theatre . . . He was the cockiest clacking cod Sean had ever
encountered, adazzle with iridescent ignorance of the drama;
a fellow who should never have been allowed even to pull up
a curtain from the stage of a tuppeny gaff . . . The play,
admittedly, was a difficult one, possibly even a bad one, but
the shocking production failed, in every possible way, to

show whether it was one, or all, of these; failed to give the slightest guidance to the experimental playwright.

The director died many years ago.

IV

About this time I had a mild nervous breakdown; mostly depression Dr Varian told me. I had no sort of outlet, no external life; a Torquay specialist agreed that I needed more gaiety. Sean liked only a few chosen guests; small talk defeated him; if I had asked the wrong people, they would naturally have wanted to see him, and if he failed to appear and said he was busy, they would have thought him unwilling or rude. One could ask only someone he was prepared to meet; an American friend or somebody close to us. Certainly not my mother, who was now lodging at Paignton: she had never been far off, and I knew by heart every peevish complaint and criticism.

The right things could happen. Thus, Bobbie (Robert) Lewis, the American director, looked in at Tingrith on a Sunday in 1949 after reading *Cock-a-doodle Dandy*, a new play in which Sean had genuine faith; my favourite as well, and George Jean Nathan's. It is a comedy of the rightful joy of life, set in an Irish village under the influence of a domineering priest. Bobbie Lewis spent a long day with us at Tingrith; Sean bubbled over in his pleasure at talking again to a real theatre-man. But where was the right backing? If Bobbie had found it, the basis of the setting might have been some excellent sketches by Breon; on leaving the Army he had resolved to use his grant at an art school instead of going to University.

Infrequently I did get to London. One visit had to be a sad parting. In October 1950, as I described in *Sean*, I went to see G.B.S. at Ayot St Lawrence in Hertfordshire just before his death; he was ninety-four, pitiably frail but speaking of death and the hereafter without any fear, simply as a fresh experience.

'If there's an Almighty, Eileen, I'll have a lot of questions to ask him,' he said in his old way. When I kissed him goodbye, I knew it must be for the last time. Two days later he died, and Sean and I mourned him deeply.

                                    V

I took care that we used our little car as much as we could; at this time it was a little Ford I had bought on hire-purchase. Because I had no money for instalments, I gradually sold my few pieces of jewellery and a fur coat Nancy Astor had given me when we stayed with her in St James's Square at the time of *Within the Gates*. In the Ford we drove to the Shakespeare Festival at Stratford-upon-Avon where Glen Byam Shaw, a friend since *The Miracle*, was co-director (on a second visit Sean went as well); and we drove to Winchester, Salisbury and Stonehenge. We would often go in the summer to the Devon sea I loved; and once, after lying awake all night worrying about it, I even drove to London. When in 1955 the actor-manager, Sam Wanamaker, sent out *Purple Dust* on tour with Miles Malleson as one of the Englishmen, Stoke, and Walter Hudd as the other, Poges, who had a hint of Billy McElroy, Sean watched the London rehearsals in a church hall off Kingsway; later we travelled to Edinburgh, an immense journey for him, to see how the production had grown. Malleson's performance, which had unaccountably lost its original vigour, disappointed us, but we did have a lively holiday and met the Scottish poet, Hugh McDiarmid, 'Alba's poet and one of Alba's first men,' to whom Sean dedicated *Sunset and Evening Star*. There was something else, most unexpected, that seemed romantic to me and highly amused Sean. The evening paper had announced that we were in Edinburgh; when we reached the theatre a note was waiting for us at the stage door. Mr Morrison, the widower who many years ago had taken me about when I was in the D'Oyly Carte, had written to ask if I still remembered him and to say how much he would like us to meet again. We did meet him, and he was as pleasant as of old. As for *Purple Dust*, even though it never reached a London theatre, it had been moving to hear such a speech as this (by a Second Workman, of all people):

. . . What is it all now but a bitther noise of cadgin' mercy from heaven, an' a sour handlin' of life for a cushioned seat in a corner? There is no shout in it; no sound of a slap of a spear in a body; no song; no sturdy winecup in a sturdy hand; no liftin' of a mighty arm to push back the tumblin' waters from a ship just sthrikin' a storm. Them that fight now fight in a daze of thradin'; for buyin' and sellin', for whores an' holiness, for th' image o' God on a golden coin; while th' men o' peace are little men now, writin' dead words with their tiny pens, seekin' a tiny and tendher way to the end. Respectable lodgers with life they are, behind solid doors with knockers on them, an' curtained glass to keep the stars from starin'.

VI

In the spring of 1954 Bobbie Lewis asked Shivaun if we would care to go to London for the first night of his production of *Teahouse of the August Moon* at Her Majesty's. Just then I had noticed an advertisement for a plan called a 'budget account' at a store in Oxford Street: you got £25 or £50 worth of goods and paid for them on a never-never scheme. It sounded highly convenient and on our first London morning we went to the store and took £40 worth, using every penny we were allowed, and buying in particular some cotton frocks that it was fashionable then to wear, very tight-waisted with a full skirt. This 'budget account' would be my undoing because as soon as I had paid up even half of what I owed, I began to buy still more stuff; my correspondence with the store went on for months.

Round this time Tom Curtiss, as Paris drama critic of the *New York Herald-Tribune*, invited me to stay at his Paris hotel with Shivaun, who was a teenager in what I called the criticism-of-mother period. So we took our new dresses and at four o'clock one afternoon arrived from the airport at Tom's hotel. Knowing nothing of teenagers, he had ordered a bottle of champagne on ice: Shivaun drank it like lemonade. I was utterly gone when we reached our room. Shivaun merely hung up her things, murmuring how dreadful mothers were: surely I couldn't have allowed so little to go to my head?

Tom took us immediately to all sorts of parties: one a sumptuous affair given by Maurice Chevalier at a restaurant in the park, two others by film directors in their opulent houses. Outwardly a demure, good-looking schoolgirl, Shivaun was too young for this; she spent the time nudging me and saying that I was either giggling too much or talking too loudly. One evening Tom had to cover an important première. Because he would not be free until eleven-thirty, he told us of a good restaurant in easy walking distance, with a cinema opposite it. We began to dress. I was wearing 'costume' jewellery – earrings and a kind of necklace, quite the thing then – but when I put on the earrings Shivaun said solemnly, 'I don't think you should wear those. You make people look at you.' I said: 'Well, Shivaun – and what have you got against me now?' To which she replied in the most distant tones, 'I don't think I've actually got anything against you; but at this age, according to Freud, I should definitely not like my mother.'

Not a good beginning. At the restaurant, when I saw the menu, I was not sure that we had money enough. Still, conversation, if a trifle stiff, was not too bad, and we managed to appear amiable with each other until I choked on a piece of steak. For a moment I could not move. Then, flinging out my arms and uttering the most extraordinary sounds, I rushed for the cloakroom. Poor Shivaun; every Freudian instinct rose, for here was her mother making a complete fool of herself in public. Gasping, I got to the cloakroom and might have died, I daresay, if an alert attendant had not pushed her finger down my throat and I was able to breathe again. Back at the table Freud

had vanished. Shivaun was so worried that she had become just
an ordinary daughter again, begging me not to talk while I was
eating. After paying an immense bill that we could just settle,
we walked over to the cinema on an even keel and happy with
each other.

Not for long. I was aware in the queue that the man behind
me was acting most embarrassingly. Shivaun had not seen it.
'Whatever are you making such a fuss about?' she said when
I dragged her to the back of the queue. 'You're all right now.'
'I don't want to go near that man!' I exclaimed. 'Oh!' she
said angrily. 'Well . . . I don't want to go to any cinema. Let's
go home.' Silently we crossed back to the hotel. Shivaun went
to bed and fell asleep; and before midnight Tom rang up to ask
what kind of an evening we had had. I said: 'Indescribable!'
Suddenly it seemed to be wildly comic.

After that night Shivaun dropped the Freudian business. Tom
invited us to coffee one morning. A friend, he told us, was
connected with the shooting of a colour film starring Robert
Mitchum, and it might be fun if Shivaun could get a small
crowd part and I were to walk on; he was going to have a line
or two himself, and since extras – whether they were needed or
not – were paid by the day, we might make quite a few francs.
Off we went to a suburban studio and signed on. Shivaun was
chosen as one of the crowd in a café scene; and in a bar scene
where we were sitting about, I had to come forward and say a
few words to Mitchum, trying not to look down at the limiting
chalk-marks as I did so. It was an amusing week: daily drives
to and from the studio, lunches on bread and cheese and wine
at a country restaurant. It could have been tedious, I suppose,
for the café scene was shot a good twenty times; but by now,
professionals all, we were enjoying it as much as we enjoyed the
pleasant sum in francs that helped us with our final shopping
at the Galeries Lafayette.

Two or three years afterwards the film, in colour, broke upon
Torquay. With Shivaun and Niall I stood in pouring rain at
the head of the queue; we got into the front row of the dress

circle and annoyed the audience by screaming 'There we are!'
and pointing when the café scene came on. My single line to
Mitchum was cut; but Tom said that when he saw the film in
London it was in, and his own line as well. Unfortunately, not
a talent scout in sight.

VII

I had another break, but at home. Robert Emmett (Bob) Ginna
had thought up a pictorial feature on Sean which, though not
commissioned at the time, appeared eventually in Life. It meant
that Bob, with Gjon Mili, arrived in Totnes to describe and
photograph Sean, his family, and his surroundings. I had been
missing our American visitors; now these two were with
us for a fortnight, and Sean could scarcely have been happier
with them: Gjon, a tall, dark Albanian, electric with vitality
and a great talker; Bob boyish and equally good-humoured. Gjon
was a stickler about his equipment, and, while generous, puri-
tanically careful with money. Young Bob was altogether more
free and easy. On the second day, Gjon discovered that a part
was missing from one of his cameras and turned to ask Bob for
the Leica he always carried. It turned out then that Bob, short
of cash, had 'hocked' it in Paris. Gjon was both shocked and
maddened, and Sean did his best to calm him.

That fortnight Sean must have walked miles: Gjon photographed him dozens of times in the lanes, on the Dartington
estate, by the river, and in Tingrith house and garden, besides
making for himself a talking film of the O'Caseys – mostly a
day of Tingrith life – which he shows even now in New York
at a big party. (I saw it at one during 1973 when they were dis-
playing Sean's manuscripts in the New York Public Library.)
After Gjon and Bob had coaxed Sean to dinner at their hotel,
they would return to sit by his fire; Gjon would recall his early
life in the mountains, and he and Sean would extol their
mothers, women of great strength of character. In Gjon's

country, if an eldest son were leaving, his mother would bathe him, give him fresh clothes and linen, and urge him in traditional terms to be upright, honest, and a true son of his father. Listening, Bob and I would drink endless cups of tea. They were days of rare companionship; I was sorry they had to end.

Fifteen years at Tingrith had to end also. Our landlord needed the house for some of his relatives; it was perfectly legal, and Sean, dreading another change, could not think of an excuse to keep us there. Deep down, even though I detested the move and its mechanics, I was not sorry to leave Totnes. Breon had chosen to study art; Niall had just been called up; Shivaun was a weekly boarder at Dartington. Tingrith was not the same place without the children coming home from school. It had been our best time; as a family we were united, and Sean was a good father, lenient and kind. He would read to Breon and Niall when they were young; and if, with his eyesight weakening, he could read only baby-books at Shivaun's bedtime, in the mornings when I was busy cleaning or cooking, he would play with her by the hour. Though occasionally I had to get off to London, go to theatres, see a little night life, and carry on with a romance or two which meant nothing, there was no doubt at all that Sean was the one person I really needed.

I did wonder about a move nearer to London – not that Sean could have faced the city itself. I would have liked it, but it was a luxury we could never have afforded. In any event, Shivaun had refused to be a full boarder, so we had to search for a home within an easy bus radius of Dartington. Eventually, after scouring through Paignton and Brixham – no joke, for I had broken my wrist, could not drive the car, and had to rely on buses – I found a flat on the highest point of St Marychurch, just beyond Torquay and looking across Petitor Downs. This was it; within a week or so the furniture vans were standing outside Tingrith.

CHAPTER FOURTEEN

The Torquay Years

BY this time need I repeat that it was a trying move? Our furniture looked sound enough if we left it alone, but it was disastrous to shift it, to expose the worn patches, the sagging
springs no one had seen when it stood quietly in the usual
place. I saw all this as chairs and sofas, beds and tables, were
carried down the path from Tingrith, and again when they
had to be taken up an outside flight of steps to the Torquay
flat. At Totnes the four men had grumbled enough about Sean's
books. At Torquay they merely stood and glared. Afraid lest
they flatly refused to lift the crates, I tried to jolly them along.
After a lot of theatrical brow-mopping to show what a strain it
was, they got the job done, and there we were: a flat on the
downs at St Marychurch, with a fine view out to sea and above
an attractive garden that belonged to the ground floor. We had
our own tiny garden at the side. Sean wrote in *Under a Colored
Cap* (1963):

St Marychurch is three hundred feet above sea-level, and the
O'Caseys' flat rises thirty or so feet higher, looking over the
tops of many trees. Twenty-two concrete steps lead to the
front door, before which stretches a concrete balcony where
I sit for many hours when the weather is good. Looking
straight before me, I can see the green cliffs of Babbacombe
guarding Babbacombe Bay; to the left, the north, on the Barton Heights, sits the village of Barton, rising in stages along
the hill so that when night comes the light of street lamps and

in the homes of the people shine out tier upon tier, reminding me whenever I glance at them of the lights of New York, making me a little sad thinking of a city I love and shall never see again.

The flat could seem crowded if we were all at home, but in those days we were seldom together. I could not foresee that here we would have both the deepest sadness in our married life and the happiness of knowing that Sean's fame had spread and that his plays were being done in Germany, France, and New York. Paul Shyre succeeded with American stage readings of *Pictures in the Hallway* and *I Knock at the Door*. Money, which had been so scarce, arrived regularly for a time, tempting me to be extravagant again with new carpets and cushions, upholstery and decoration.

When I was driving in from St Marychurch not long after our move, I spotted a nursery garden that sold plants and flowers and had a wide grass path at its centre. It looked inviting. I spoke to the owner, a countryman from Norfolk named Geoffrey Dobbie, and bought plants from him; and he suggested, on bringing them round, that he put them in himself. Getting to know Sean, as interested as he was in flowers and birds, he grew into a valuable friend: so much so that if I were away briefly in London, as sometimes I had to be, Sean would let Geoffrey get an evening meal for him, a task forbidden to our daily girl.

Sean was profoundly interested in nature, often swearing at his poor sight because he could not watch the birds more closely. This was among several things that he and Brooks Atkinson, the American drama critic, had in common, and when he was writing to Brooks, he would describe anything new he had observed in the garden or in the country. There was a crow that had lost a leg. When Sean sat on the balcony of our flat, the bird would perch on the edge of his chair, or on the balcony railing, while Sean fed him.

II

Immediately we reached Torquay we were in action: the American television people, N.B.C., scheduled an O'Casey film for a series called 'Elder Wise Men'. We knew the interviewer, Bob Ginna (from *Life* magazine), and Bob (Robert D.) Graff, the producer; the cameraman, Wolfgang Suschitzky ('Su'), became another dear friend. Sean started doubtfully; but, aware that the money would help, ceased to be nervous and joined in with relish. No need to ask me: I welcomed any activity and life. Geoffrey brought boxes of petunias to brighten our steps and the entrance to the flat, and the flowers made a neat excuse for Sean's opening lines.

Originally, Ginna and Graff had not meant to disturb the home. It would be just as convenient, they told me encouragingly, to fix up a set in a hotel room, to furnish it like Sean's, and to take across some of his books. In effect, it would be a film set: a bad idea, for Sean would feel self-conscious and unnatural. Why not use the flat, I suggested, and concentrate on Sean's own room which so exactly framed his personality? I couldn't have known what I was saying. At once a huge van blocked the drive; the flat was turned into a studio; all over it they scattered cameras and electric equipment; and the family was on hand to 'feed' the star, who was Sean, of course. I thought, though, in the playback of our brief scene, grouped at the tea-table, we did sound a little odd. Ordinarily, I dined out with the two Bobs and Su, while Sean, tired after a day of takes and re-takes, would have his quiet meal at home. Innately an actor, he had as cheerful a time as we did. At the end of the film, answering Bob Ginna's question, 'After these many years, what have you found about life? What do you really believe now?' he said this:

But what is life? Ah, well, that's a question similar to the one Captain Boyle put to Joxer. You know: 'What is the stars, Joxer? What is the stars? That's the question!' What is life, Bob, what is life? . . . Well, I have found life an enjoyable, enchanting, active, and sometimes a terrifying experience; and I've enjoyed it completely. A lament in one ear, maybe; but always a song in the other. And to me life is simply an invitation to live.

Probably Christmas 1954 was as happy as any since the children grew up: everyone there, an old-fashioned get-together, carols at the piano, Niall (who loved Christmas) taking endless trouble over a wine-cup. But on Christmas Day Sean was not really himself; that evening he kept having to rest. In the New Year, when we were alone again, they sent him into Torquay Hospital where he had two operations, contracted pneumonia, and remained for eight or nine weeks. Breon hurried down to stay with me. It was ghastly weather with thick snow, one of the few years when snow in Torquay was deep. Most days I visited Sean twice; in convalescence I took along his letters and tried to keep him going; he would see no one else but the children, detested hospital life, and longed as ever for his own room. Each of us did have a mild romantic side-line. Sean could still pick a good-looking girl; there were several among the nurses and he took a shine, as we say, to the Sister on the ward, young for her rank, who often stopped to chat before going off duty. I fell instantly for the surgeon, a handsome man; a gentle flirtation brightened things, and I would rush to get there whenever he was due to visit Sean.

Sean was very frail on leaving hospital. He had lost so much weight that he appeared to have shrunk; and he never recovered his full vitality. Otherwise he walked well and his mind was sharp. I was accustomed to a man who had never been in good health, and it did not fully occur to me that he was ageing; he was seventy-six.

We had chosen St Marychurch largely to be within reach of Shivaun. But when nearly seventeen she was accepted for a London art school, left Dartington, and found digs opposite the flat where Niall lived in Abbey Gardens. After a term or so she decided to transfer to R.A.D.A., the drama school near London University where Niall was, and they spent a great deal of time with each other. Breon, who had come home to paint, found it so frustrating to be packed into one room that he first rented an attic studio in a Torquay mews and then turned towards Cornwall and the artists' colony at St Ives. Engagingly, he told me I would be better than he was at discovering a studio, so, with a friend, I went down and encountered a severely puritanical estate agent. Certainly there was a studio, very large and cold and not meant for sleeping.

'Now,' began the agent, 'is he the type that gives parties?'

'No,' I said.

Here he awarded us each an acid-drop from a sticky bag. 'Does he play a lot of loud records?'

'No,' I said.

'He wouldn't be giving drinking parties, would he?'

'No,' I said. 'I don't think he could afford it even if he wanted to.'

We had been as ingratiating as possible, and it was five-thirty in the afternoon. Where, the man asked, were we staying? He hoped at a café; at least a temperance hotel. My friend had the sense to say, 'Perhaps you could give us a nice address?' He could; we took the nice address of a café that let rooms and said with much gratitude that we would try it. We would call next morning to sign the agreement. Wishing him goodbye on the main road, we slipped into the small hotel where we had already booked, relaxed over a stiff drink, and hoped he had not seen us. Apparently not. Breon got the large studio at a very low rent, and in St Ives later he married and settled down.

My mother, all this while, had been about Torquay in rooms. Getting on for ninety, progressively awkward, she kept the ancient ritual of changing her address nearly every fortnight. I would tear round to her in the car, a Hillman now, during Sean's rest. Could I possibly get back to make his tea before he woke? She was still drinking – her way of roaming off into a fantasy-world, and torture for me. I recall her landlady, one of the series, telephoning on a hot summer Bank Holiday, 'Mrs O'Casey, you must come over to see your mother.' She was well away when I arrived. The landlady, she said, was awful. The place was awful. She was very ill. I must get her out at once. Actually I got her to bed and looked longingly through the window at the sunshine. Listening to her useless talk, I was sorry for her but sorrier for myself. I appeared to have been listening for ever to the same litany of complaints and wondering when in God's name it would end. At length I left her, putting on the table the small bottle of brandy I had been cautious enough to bring; without it I knew she would stagger out somehow to find one.

Walking with Sean that evening, and raging inwardly at the injustice of it all, I had no chance to talk; my mother was never his subject and he could not endure her. But gradually I relaxed. When we came in we probably listened, as so often, to a radio programme or to a television play, though for Sean by then it had become barely a shadow-show on the large-scale set we had hired.

III

It was Christmas 1956. Niall I had seen in London on and off that autumn, excessively pale and run down, perhaps trying to do too much; he fitted into his days everything he could, many external things besides his work at the University. Thus he played the trumpet in a jazz band; simply for a party he might travel to Devon in an old Ford van and be back at his classes next morning. Apart from the pallor, he had been his lively self until, a week before Christmas, he drove home with Shivaun. It was the saddest Christmas in our lives.

When Niall arrived he looked so tired that I persuaded him to see our Dr Doran who examined him and said he would like to bring a specialist at once. They were with Niall for a long time. Then they came to me, alone in the front room, with the dreadful news that he had leukaemia and that there was no hope of recovery. It was beyond any of us, certainly Niall himself, to understand. Even now, I can feel the icy chill that ran through me.

After this it was a long nightmare. I travelled with Niall in the ambulance to an Exeter hospital, staying in a hotel close by; everywhere carol-singing, Christmas trees lighted, hotel bars crowded. I felt as if I were walking in a dream, utterly detached, with my sorrow and my hope: I continued to hope, and would not believe otherwise. Sean, Breon, and Shivaun arrived on Christmas Eve, and all I can say is that we got through the days somehow. I was with Niall nearly all the time. On Christmas Day we went to see him. Ill as he was, he was able to talk; his Christmas cards were on the locker and he managed to joke about some of them. We even gave each other our presents. I can still picture Sean and Shivaun as they went slowly from the ward, quite unaware that they would never see Niall again. The memory can fill me to the brim with sorrow.

The expert on leukaemia, Dr Bodley Scott, was at St Bartholomew's in London; now Dr Doran said that Niall must go there as soon as possible. Though it was not easy to convince the hospital doctor that the move was essential, we went up two days after Christmas. They took Niall by ambulance to the station and I can hear him saying, 'How wonderful to be in the fresh air again!' It was raining gently, and he felt a few drops on his face and smiled with the joy of it, the joy of life. Bart's did give us hope. I was allowed to remain all day with him. After a few days he was able to walk to the bathroom, and I see clearly, so often, that tall, handsome boy, twenty years old, as he moved down the ward. There was hope then in both our hearts.

Breon was with me now; Shivaun had the lonely task of watching Sean. Vainly we hoped Niall might have a reprieve, a year or more, something not unknown with leukaemia; but on the last night when he grew worse and they took away the tubes which had been attached to his arm, he knew and I knew

that it was the end. I have written about this before,* and I
cannot repeat it. Death's finality is fearful. How I moved away
from Niall I cannot say. Breon was my strength; in the days
that followed he dealt with the stream of formal questions that
makes you wonder how an unendurable loss that has dulled
some part of you for ever can be simply a thing of routine for
a recording clerk.

Niall was cremated at Golders Green. Back in Torquay I had
to try to console Shivaun and Sean. Soon Breon went back to
St Ives, Shivaun to her drama school, and Sean and I were alone.
We were both in a desperate state; I managed to get through
the days but the evenings were intolerable, and it was weeks
before we really managed to be normal and knew we had to go
on living.

On a quiet afternoon some years later a man I did not recognise rang our doorbell. He looked so distracted that I had to ask
him in, and when he told me his name I remembered at once
that Christmas in the Exeter hospital, Niall's doctor, and our
momentary conflict. In a broken voice he said that he was in
great distress: his young son, while swimming that morning,
had struck his head against a rock and had been drowned. The
doctor was overwhelmed. 'Mrs O'Casey,' he said, 'I had to come
to you. I have never forgotten how you were when your son
Niall was dying of leukaemia.' Taking him in to Sean, who did
not know him at first, I explained the tragic circumstances. We
talked together for half an hour in the fullest warmth and
sympathy and I thought once more how ironical life could be.
When the doctor had left us we never saw him again.

IV

Now the days in Torquay weighed heavily, but I had to be
with Sean and I would not run from memories. Sean was settled
in his room that faced the hills, or on the balcony, where in

* In *Sean*.

warm weather he could rest among the flowering plants he loved, the hydrangea and fuchsia and heliotrope. Even if life was so frustrating, to move now would be impossible and selfish. But what was there in Torquay? No real theatre; concerts occasionally, sometimes the Bournemouth Symphony Orchestra; popular films (not often a foreign one). Sybil Thorndike came down to the Pavilion with Lewis Casson and I was ashamed to see so small a house. The Cassons called on us that week; it touched me to hear Sybil talking to Sean, who greatly admired her, and to watch their shared affection. Thirty years before, and new to London, Sean had seen her in *Saint Joan*. He wrote to one of his Irish friends: 'Great buttie now of Sybil Thorndike; very natural, kind and lovable.'

Friends invited me occasionally to a local restaurant. A Wine and Dine Society had functions perhaps twice a year, but you could not help feeling that you were 'tacked on' to your friendly hosts; you could hardly be at ease without a companion of your own, and I gave up going. It was not very sensible to leave Sean by himself and to feel lonely at a party. Saturday morning was the week's relief; whatever the season or the weather, shine or hail, only illness would stop me going to one of the two fashionable teashops where Torquay met for gossip and coffee. You dressed up for this – there was a touch of the gaily competitive. During the summer visits from students would keep us going: doubtless too many of these, but it was hard to excuse yourself to such eager young people, often American or European. You felt that you were keeping them deliberately out of Sean's way, an implication I hated whether they called at the door or merely telephoned.

The telephone had its pleasures. A London newspaper correspondent used to chat to Sean in Gaelic; and he had several long and exuberant talks with Brendan Behan, who always acknowledged his influence. 'You ought to go easy with the drink, Brendan,' Sean would say; they never met because people had warned me that Brendan would get really tight and that was something Sean never forgave.

If anyone had told me that I would be having telephone talks with Sean from America, I might have shrugged it off as moonshine. But, astonishingly, I was in New York again – thirty-two years after that morning when Cohan watched me sail in the *Mauretania*, my mind full of London and *Juno*. Now it was the autumn of 1958. Paul Shyre was to direct *Cock-a-doodle Dandy* off Broadway and to play the 'very wise old crawthumper'; and Cheryl Crawford was doing the *Gunman* on Broadway itself. Would Sean be there? they asked; two openings in one week, expenses paid. Dr Doran shook his head; the journey and the entertaining might be risky. Sean never even considered it, and when Brooks Atkinson wrote to us, 'Why not let Eileen come alone?' he was delighted. It was time for an O'Casey to go. Though Cheryl Crawford was not too ready to pay for me without Sean, Lucille Lortel, who backed *Cock-a-doodle Dandy*, offered both fare and expenses, a wonderful break. We had more money coming in; I got an elegant evening coat from John Cavanagh, the dress designer, whose mother and my own were born at the same town in County Mayo – and it was all as suddenly exciting as my theatre days before marriage. Once Breon had come to stay with Sean, I flew off on a trip that fulfilled every hope. In Brooks Atkinson's company I admired the opening of the *Gunman*, and if *Cock-a-doodle Dandy* was less fortunate, nothing blurred New York's affection for Sean. I met such people, tirelessly generous, as S.Y. (Yip) Harburg, librettist of *Finian's Rainbow*, the Atkinsons, Richard Watts junior, Lucille Lortel and her husband Louis Schweitzer, Bob Graff, Julie Haydon, Cathy Fannon. The lights of Broadway reminded me of my impressionable days; Central Park spread grandly below my hotel windows; and I dined at the Algonquin where the foyer seemed to be unchanged. It was a great return; reluctant to leave, I was still anxious to get back to the family, though Niall – I knew with a pang – would not be there.

v

One evening in Torquay I was summoned urgently to my
mother. Losing her balance, she had fallen backwards down the
stair, splitting her head open; they laid her on a sofa until the
doctor came, and she was carried to bed, undressed gently, and
given a pain-killing injection. She would not live through the
night.

When I reached her she was exceedingly weak but conscious.
'Eileen,' she said, 'you have been good to me. I think I am
surely dying . . . I have not had a happy life.' I persuaded her
not to talk; all I could do was to moisten her lips with brandy
now and then until the doctor hurried in for a fresh injection.
Trying though she had been, he recognised her courage, and
he said (as others had), 'What a waste of a good brain!' The
idea of death terrified her; I said gently that, as an ardent
Catholic all her life, she had no cause to fear. This may have
consoled her. She begged for a priest; the last Sacraments did
calm her mind, and in the early hours, quietly and at rest, she
died.

I felt sorrier for her on her deathbed than ever in her life, yet
in honesty a burden had dropped. I arranged for a Mass at the
Catholic Church, and for the funeral (the first of its kind I had
known); the only other mourners were Geoffrey Dobbie, whom
Sean had asked to accompany me, and my mother's landlady,
Mrs Davies. Snow covered the ground that afternoon. Both the
uphill road and the cemetery paths were icy: perilous for the
hearse, and for the mourners as they walked to the grave. When
I bent over it to put earth on the coffin, a chilling experience, I
stumbled on the slippery grass and would have fallen over the
edge if Mrs Davies had not caught my arm. Flowers had come
from Ireland, but I was the only one of her people who could be
near my mother at the end, and the extreme loneliness of the
funeral saddened me.

In her last few years my mother had been less troubled. We

were better off; I saw that she had her own rugs and curtains and her personal photographs around her, and I was able to get an amusing driver, known to many Torquay old ladies, to take her about in his ancient car. Really it was not until I sorted her things that I knew what a character she had been, how clever in dealing with such people as the Gentlewomen's Society and the Catholic Society to help widows. They had dispatched many parcels of clothing to her, dressing-gowns, bedroom slippers, and so forth, all in excellent condition; she had to be 'well turned out', and if by any chance she thought a garment was unworthy of her, she did not hesitate to send it back with a polite note. No wonder her parcels were hand-picked. She had a small pension; and every week I had given her enough for the rent and more – Sean's money, but he had never grumbled about it even when we were so hard up ourselves. More than ever I understood how lonely she was: largely her own fault, if we can say such a thing about the way one is brought up. Here it began in childhood: her Irish family were well-to-do middle-class folk and she never liked mixing with people 'beneath' her, a period inhibition that simply added to her loneliness. By her own lights she did her best for me; and she held that it was both a tradition and a duty that children should care for their mothers in old age.

VI

Quite often now, and it was never a chore, I had to run up to London about Sean's productions. More money was reaching us from America, so instead of staying at hotels I took, at a controlled rent, a tiny flat in Cromwell Road, empty because its tenant had been killed in a car accident. Behind a large block, in a mews, and up some iron steps, it had two rooms, a corridor-kitchen, and a bathroom. Ideal for me; Sean, who liked it, saw it only once. That was when he travelled to London in 1959 for *Cock-a-doodle Dandy* at the Royal Court: not a major production, but he was glad, at least ten years after it was published, to see his favourite play on the stage. I cannot say we heard it all, for Wilfrid Lawson's Sailor Mahan was oddly indistinct.

That Christmas we were with Shivaun. A lot had been happening to her. Four or five months after Niall died, she had joined a group of Irish players on an American college tour, and we missed her badly – her telephone talks from London, her occasional week-ends, and her near-professional haircutting for Sean who hated having to go to a barber. The long tour had taken her as far as Mexico; when she landed from the boat at Plymouth I brought her home by car with her bundles and baskets, her large trunk, the coloured shirts she had found in Mexico for Sean and Breon, and the rugs and wooden bowls, the beads and jewellery for me. Soon she got a job in the design workshops of the Bristol Old Vic, and stayed for two years. Sean and I, who had hated Christmas after Niall's death, spent it at Bristol in 1959, seeing the Slade-Reynolds musical Shivaun had helped to design: a change, but Christmas must be a time for memories. Nowadays I want to get it over.

Breon and his wife Doreen often visited us from Cornwall – with five-year-old Alison, Doreen's daughter by her first husband, then with Breon's eldest child Oona as a baby, and later with Duibhne who was a year younger. Sean was very fond of them. His essays, Under a Colored Cap, are dedicated to 'little Alison and littler Oona: to be read when the sturdier airs of womanhood flow round them – should they then desire to do so.' I do regret that he saw neither Breon's young son Brendan nor Shivaun's son Ruben: he would have been very proud of them.

Another visitor was the famous Irish actor, Barry Fitzgerald. He came to make, with Sean, a scene for a film of the Abbey Theatre's history, and when Barry entered the room they could hardly speak for joy at the reunion. At Barry's death, Sean, as the first to recognise his talent, was lovingly remembered in his will. Bernard and Josephine Miles, who were staging The Bishop's Bonfire at their Mermaid Theatre in London, also came down to us. Bernard had brought a tape-recorder for Sean's ideas, a simple machine that even I could work. I imagined that if we could have one ourselves, Sean might be helped through an evening by recording his thoughts or describing some of the events in his life. His sight was gravely worse. Without reading, so essential to him, he was lost. Again and again I would see him struggling, holding a book at a strange slant, peering at it patiently from the corner of an eye as he tried for five or ten minutes to get the print into focus. The recorder Bernard sent down did divert him sometimes. Though he never completely relaxed, treating it instinctively as a performance, he managed to make half-a-dozen personal tapes.

He needed me so much that I lost any desire to go away. On his eightieth birthday it startled him to get telegrams and cablegrams from all over the world – the Continent, America, the U.S.S.R. – as well as a host of flowers, a bunch of eighty red roses from Mary O'Malley of the Lyric, Belfast, and another from Joan Littlewood, of Theatre Workshop. Surprised though he was, I don't say that he showed his excitement, but I knew how deeply pleased he was at heart. I bought him a bright poloneck sweater, and we had our customary day on our own and our usual tea; no birthday cake, but I did give him a nice new pipe. He had never kept anniversaries. When the children were young he could have scarcely ignored the preparations and parties, and very likely the film show (in those days we had a projector), but he would always have to be reminded of my own birthday, which is two days after Christmas and was a pale affair even when I was a child. At Christmas itself, when he wanted to give me something, shopping was out of the question. He never knew what in heaven's name I might like, so again he had to ask the children to choose. Obviously I enjoyed flowers or presents, but I understood Sean's attitude: it was neither lack of affection nor generosity – he had one of the most generous natures I knew. The plain fact was that for the first forty years of his life anniversaries had meant nothing whatever.

VII

In 1960 he published his last full-length work, 'an idle laughing play/About the things encumbering Ireland's way.' It was entitled *The Drums of Father Ned; or, A Mickrocosm of Ireland* (originally *The Night Is Whispering*). Among his best-natured and most harmless plays, it was a mystery to me why the Irish banned it. Three short pieces had still to appear; also the essays in *Under a Colored Cap* – the name, in its American spelling, from a coloured felt cap, a 'beano', he had worn habitually since Shivaun made one for him as a schoolgirl. Bob Graff proposed to buy the six books of autobiography for a filmed life. Sean and I differed about this. I believed that nothing of the sort should be done while a man was alive. But Sean accepted the offer; he was relieved to know I should be better provided for, with a sum to be paid, according to contract, over three years. The film, made in Dublin and entitled *Young Cassidy*, with an unsatisfactory script by the dramatist John Whiting, had a variety of setbacks during its casting and production; Sean, who read little now, was far too ill and tired to think about it earnestly and it was not a success when released after his death. Shivaun had a small part in it as Lady Gregory's maid at Coole.

Right to his last weeks Sean was indomitable, answering David Krause's detailed queries for a full-scale edition of the letters, or allowing Gjon Mili – who was over at Dartington and had asked for a picture session – to photograph him all round the flat, sitting and standing. I had protested at this, but Sean wanted it, and, in spite of his fatigue, it appeared to do him good. Looking back, I think Sean's wish to see both Gjon and Dave when he was so frail and weary, was a kind of premonition.

Let me end this chapter with his own words. Back in 1936, when he was drafting a talk to undergraduates at Cambridge, he wrote: 'Often in Dublin, wandering about the streets, I have looked up at the beautiful and graceful façade of Trin

Coll and have wondered what beautiful mysteries of happy life were going on inside of the building . . . Occasionally I have seen a solemn-faced young man going with books in his hand or under his arm and have wondered on what tremendous things his mind was concentrating. Afterwards I have concluded that his mind may have been full of thoughts about a girl, but a young girl to a young man is a wonderful thing to think about.' A quarter of a century went by during which he was offered and politely rejected several honours. Then, in the spring of 1961, Trinity College, Dublin, suggested an honorary doctorate, and he answered in a letter that has never been published. Here it is:

> Flat 3, Trumlands Road,
> St Marychurch,
> Torquay, Devon.
> 4 February 1961.

J. P. Mitchell, Esq.,
Registrar,
Trinity College, Dublin.

Dear Mr Mitchell,
It was indeed a generous idea on the part of your Board to wish to lift me into a Degree of a Doctor in Letters, and I am grateful to them.

It would be an odd thing for me who as a youngster used to admire the clock on the façade with its blue face and golden hands, but wouldn't venture within the railings, [if I] should now go in, and come out wearing the hood of a fine and honouring Degree.

I have always fought against any privilege of class or wealth preventing the brighter minds of all people from free entry into Universities, so as to ensure for them a fuller development from the knowledge of scholarship and the interchange of ideas through association with fellow-students, and do so still.

Sean O'Casey, Litt.D.! No, sir, this would never do.

I am a wandering minstrel singing his share of songs at the corners of occasional streets: such I was, such I am, and such I shall die.

I am sure that the Members of your Board and you will understand this, and think it a fair reason for refusing your Board's generous offer of a great and unexpected honour.

On my part, may I offer my deep and best wishes to your famous University this year and for all the years to come? Wishes which come from the heart out.

Yours very sincerely,
SEAN O'CASEY

CHAPTER FIFTEEN

Beginning Again

DOCTOR DORAN had said to me, 'Eileen, you must realise Sean will not go on for ever. Maybe another few years.' During the late summer of 1964 he had been in a Torquay nursing-home with acute bronchitis. At home he was increasingly tired. We were alone in the flat; Breon was at St Ives, Shivaun acting in *Young Cassidy* in Dublin. Readily, Geoffrey Dobbie came to help and sometimes remained overnight; when Sean needed attention every four hours I had to have an alarm to wake me, and Geoffrey would stay the odd night to let me sleep.

Early in the morning of 18 September Sean's nose bled violently and at once I drove him over to Dr Doran's surgery. Doran told me to be certain that he rested. Though going on holiday himself, he said that the new partner in the practice, Dr Haskins, who was a nose, ear and throat specialist, would be on call.

We returned to the flat and Sean rested on his divan. I read to him, on and off, from Shakespeare's sonnets and his other favourite poems; and we talked of our lives together through nearly forty years: of our marriage, a risk we had both taken, a force neither of us could resist; of the good times and the hard times; and of our children. Niall we only mentioned but the bond of our loss was there. For almost the first time since we were married Sean mentioned Lee's name, passing over it quickly: 'I wonder,' he said, 'if I did right to take you from Lee?' He began to talk about the future, urging me to take care for myself. Where should I live? Perhaps in America where we had so many friends. I did not take this very seriously then; but now I see he must have had a very strong premonition of his death. This day when we were so close in our love and companionship was the more valuable to me as a memory afterwards.

At two o'clock he had his first thrombosis, an agony of pain that seemed to be in his side. Dr Haskins (who had not known Sean's case-history) arrived at once, gave an injection, and plugged his nose which had again started to bleed. Within an hour the agony returned, and he had a further injection. Holding his hand, I rode with him in an ambulance to the nursing-home. When we reached it, they carried Sean in and laid him upon the bed in a ground-floor room, but he did not stir. On the journey he had died very peacefully, the end of a wonderful life; and I felt once more that awful chill of loss. Oh, Sean, how lonely it was going to be without him!

Dr Haskins drove me home. I was not crying. If I am desperately shocked or grieved, I remain still and silent; so it was now. Going into Sean's room was fearful, yet I sat on there through the hours. Seeing his coat hanging behind the door, his boots by the fireside, his pipes, the papers scattered on the table, and in the typewriter even a page of his last article, it was impossible to imagine that he had gone. My first thought was to ring the children. Shivaun came from London, Breon from St Ives. We needed to be entirely alone: this was our personal loss and no one but ourselves could help. Every morning we drove somewhere in the Devon country, getting back at night; slowly the days passed. After Niall's death it had taken me a long time to make sense of it all: he had had no chance of fulfilment, his ambitions went with him, and his loss left a sharp physical pain. I had now to remind myself that Sean had filled every minute of his eighty-four years. Though his brain was alert and untouched, he had become nearly blind and he would never have endured more.

II

There is the thinnest of lines between grief and laughter. Sean knew it, as his plays prove. On the night before the cremation I realised that I must wear a hat in the chapel. The only one I had, a black fur, would have been conspicuous, so Shivaun altered it for me. I tried it on, and suddenly for no reason began to giggle. Breon picked it up next, exclaiming, 'I'd better wear it, Eileen, and look like Sean's daft son.' There we were, laughing hysterically on the edge of tears. Next day, at the ceremony, we had to repeat a prayer in unison, something like 'Our Father'. Halfway through it I went a line ahead, and the clergyman never caught up with me; my 'Amen' came in just before his, and I heard Shivaun giggling helplessly. No lack of grief; again simply the thinnest of lines that separated it from laughter.

Two duties were immediate. Sean's ashes must go, as he had wished, with Niall's at Golders Green; that was my first obligation. At the time my Cromwell Road flat was in a muddle; Shivaun was living in it, planning with an actor-friend another tour of American colleges. But I knew an admirer of Sean, an American writer, Lester Cole, who lived not far off and who had gone to hospital with heart trouble. He told me to use his own flat; and who should I find in it but dear Mrs Earle whom I had recommended to him as a daily help? It was a blessing, for the tranquillisers I had to take were leaving me strangely vague. I had not realised how Sean had been my whole existence. It was impossible to feel natural; at one moment I had great plans for a new life, and at the next I was quite unable to go on.

Shivaun went with me to the crematorium and to what we had assumed would be a matter of form. Sidney Bernstein, an old friend of Sean's and mine, who had telephoned to ask what he could do, had lent his car and chauffeur for my first weeks in London; and we drove out to Golders Green, Shivaun with me at the back and the chauffeur's radio music on at full pitch,

G

though we barely noticed it. At the crematorium an official took us to a room where we had to wait quite a while before two other men appeared, one in a cassock, the other bearing a small casket. Following them, as we were told, and feeling chilled, we reached some open ground and stood aside while one man held the casket and the other took the ashes from it and scattered them to the wind. I felt myself going faint; Shivaun was just as white. We had to step back to a bench and recover ourselves before walking away slowly and in silence. At the office I had to sign some papers; neither of us could speak. Then we found the car, and the driver, who had stopped playing his radio – for the sight of us would have shocked anyone – drove us to Hampstead and to the invariable selfless understanding of my friend Ella Stewart.

III

My second duty was to sell Sean's papers. He had impressed on me for six months that they were the most valuable things he could leave. I had wondered whether he might be dramatising the situation a little ('not having long to live'). Now, recalling his wishes, I had to have everything sorted and listed, a task for which he had named Ronald Ayling, who had visited him in student days. It was ironical to me that these papers and scribbled notes should have become so valuable because the man who wrote them had died. I thought of the many papers we had thrown away during our moves. We should never have been as careful as we were if G.B.S., on one of my visits, had not impressed on me that I must keep every note that Sean had scribbled and put them together – in drawers, in cardboard boxes, anywhere, so long as they were preserved.

After Ron, who was lecturing at Bristol University, had finished a most intricate job, I carried the papers to London. They were placed in the Macmillan safe, a huge, frigid vault with a heavy fireproof door which when you were there had to be held securely open – sometimes I wondered whether it might bang shut at a vital moment and leave me to freeze or suffocate to death beside my legacy. Several places wanted to buy the papers – the British Museum and the University of Texas were among them – but in the end we had no qualms at all about selling to the highest bidder, the New York Public Library. Americans had always been loyal to Sean, and students would find the collection readily accessible.

The flat next. I had to pack up everything and store the furniture. Other than this, no plans: merely a need to escape from Torquay and its associations. What furniture should I get rid of? This perplexed me, for at times like these – though it ought not to matter – you do give or throw away things that one day you regret. Books, for example: I wanted to keep for myself and the children the bulk of Sean's library, so much a part of him. Geoffrey Dobbie, at sea here, did his best; Mr Tripp (a relative of the actress June), from the flat below, was more systematic. To get a permanent record of Sean's room the American photographer, Erich Hartmann, spent two days on a group of movingly atmospheric pictures: the boots by the fireplace, the coats, the waiting typewriter.

Finally, on a morning in October, the furniture gone and the rooms empty, I stood for a long time, recalling ten years of happiness and sadness; looking at the coloured doors in the kitchen that Breon had painted when Sean was in hospital and we were trying to get through the days; the bathroom with the wallpaper we had managed to hang without sticking to the walls ourselves; and the long end-to-end bookcase Breon had built in the front room. All the ideas one had put one's heart into – all gone. Shutting the door and saying farewell to that part of my life, I stepped into the cab for Torquay Station.

IV

Shivaun was about to leave for America. My former host, Lester Cole, who was now out of hospital, took me to theatres and restaurants or to meals in his flat. On tranquillisers still, I was poor company and at the theatre might drop asleep halfway through the show. Anxious about Shivaun's project, we went together to Croydon to see a spirited try-out of *The Beggar's Opera* and Sean's *Figuro in the Night*, the amusing short play he had 'prayerfully and solemnly dedicated to what is known as the ferocious chastity of Ireland'.

After Shivaun had gone I found myself relying more upon Lester. But his heart was worrying him and he had to return to America and his family for another operation, leaving me grateful for his unobtrusive and practical sympathy. Loneliness took over. At times I wondered why I was doing anything at all, and what it mattered, though behind this I did realise that I must carry on and find a larger flat for Sean's books. Roaming through vacant flats is a pretty tedious business. Some were dreary, some expensive, more just ugly. I was a dreary figure myself and over-sensitive. If I rang a friend and got the reply, 'Oh, darling, I *am* sorry, but this evening I'm going out – what about another one?' I would say 'No, I'm out all this week,' feeling at once that I was unwanted and could only be a nuisance. It was painfully easy to make a habit of not going anywhere unless the person insisted. On most evenings I ate at a little restaurant off Brompton Road. A surprising number of people did eat by themselves at night; and, for something to do, I chatted with a woman at the next table who worked, I think, in the Oriental Department of the Victoria and Albert Museum and knew what she was talking about. Her home, I gathered, was in Kent; we planned to meet regularly and to share a table. Living by herself, she had no wish for people – something extra-ordinary to me. We talked, as a rule, of everyday things, or she might describe places she had known abroad. I never heard her name; and, obsessed with a fear that she might sympathise with me, I never told her mine.

My behaviour, letting friends think that I was busy, and afraid that they were just sorry for me, could have been an echo of the convent years. In effect, it was Eileen Reynolds coming back to boast of her wonderful holidays when she had been all the time with her mother somewhere in Fulham, or had had to refuse an invitation for want of the right clothes.

One throw-back: a figure from my distant past, Esme Berkeley, was living near Richmond at a home for officers. I visited him there. An invalid, about ninety years old, he was excited to see me again and enjoyed introducing me to his nurses as Mrs Sean O'Casey. I could remind him of London in the twenties, of Stella, and of his brother Roland who had died. His father had been a general. Both the sons, always jealous of each other, were expected to enter the army, but Roland preferred banking. He was much richer than Esme who, in old age, was troubled simply because he would leave less than Roland had done. I am afraid I found this very funny.

V

I did get my flat. It was in Drayton Gardens, Kensington, a newly-converted Georgian house with a historic background. Boards outside it advertised 'Luxury Flats' which, being interpreted, meant flats with any type of bathroom. Mine on the second floor – ready in three weeks, they said brightly – had a large front room beautifully shaped, a bedroom, built-in wardrobes, a bathroom with shower, and a small kitchen. At least it had had these originally. While it was being converted the building remained open all day and the front door all night, an invitation to any passing collector. Bathroom taps, showers, and lavatory fittings were torn out roughly and removed. Between seeing the flat and living in it I had come down to a most indifferent lavatory and bath (and no shower).

On the day of my move the London *Evening News* carried an article, with photographs, announcing that Sean O'Casey's widow had bought an old Georgian house in Drayton Gardens; its entire history followed. In fact, Eileen O'Casey had rented a two-roomed flat in Drayton Gardens; but the article brought a rush of telephone calls, as well as down-and-outs at the door, all wanting me to help them before anyone saw what a small part of the building I really had.

For a while I was the sole tenant. The other three flats were vacant – it bothered me at night to go into the house and creep up in the silence. Because there had been such a number of burglaries in the district that no company would insure me without safety locks, I went to a firm that put in so many special devices you might have thought I had the Crown Jewels under my bed. Unless I was going out for a long time I did not need a key that worked the big and complex burglar-lock, but I carried it out with me when I was still the only person in the building. I am, alas, a key-loser; I lost this one on my grand-daughter Oona's birthday. I had promised to telephone her at St Ives at six o'clock, and though she might not have noticed, I was anxious to keep my word. Here I was without any keys, and nobody in the house, only empty flats.

Never mind: the telephones were already connected. I went to the flat below mine, rang Oona and eventually the police. They advised me to get on to a locksmith. I dialled the number they gave me; before long a small, wizened man appeared, performed magically with wire, and within five minutes had my door open. Relieved and thankful, I asked him in for a drink.

'Please, madam,' he said, 'tea only; I am redeemed and do not drink now.'

Mildly surprised, I made tea for us both, and he was refreshed enough to tell me proudly that he could open any safe or any lock.

'How is that?' I asked.

'Well, madam, you see I have been in.'

'In? In where?'

'In prison, madam.'

'Oh really,' I said. 'How interesting!'

'Yes, madam, I was a good safe-breaker, one of the best . . . Now I am a converted and redeemed man. Never, never again. Today I had a job at a jeweller's – '

'A jeweller's?'

'I opened their safe for them, madam.'

'Surely,' I said, 'it must have been tempting when you saw all those jewels?'

'No, madam, I am completely converted. Though, mind you, as an expert, I am very, very well paid . . .'

With this the converted safe-opener left me. I was rather sorry.

Soon the ground-floor flat was let, then the others. I was lucky, for the bottom flat went to an American girl, Mary Jenkins, who worked on the English side of a first-class American quarterly. I got to know her and Chris well, and now they are in New York I see them and their two small sons when I go over. Right below me in Drayton Gardens lived an American employed by a New York record company. So in a few weeks I had new friends – people, too, who had heard of Sean. Chris Jenkins was an efficient amateur locksmith. Though I took care not to use the big key when I was absent for a day or so, many times my neighbours had to come up with knives to prise the small Yale open. This was where Chris was skilful. He did not find it too hard – the door was badly hung.

One night Tom Curtiss, who was over from Paris and seeing me home after we had dined, came in for coffee. No key. Living above me in the penthouse flat was Julian Glover, the actor; as it was about eleven o'clock I rang his bell and asked if he would mind going down the fire-escape and through my kitchen window to open the door. Though he was in a white towelling dressing-gown he responded helpfully. Five minutes later he opened my flat door from the inside. I held it open; he vanished upstairs to his own flat; I let my door go again, it banged shut, and we were locked out. Once more I rang the bell. Once more, less graciously, Julian did his act; the fire-escape was rather sooty and his dressing-gown had begun to show it. This time I did stand firmly in the doorway. Julian simply said, and I could hardly blame him, 'Are you tight – or what?' Tom, a very sober person, was shocked.

VI

Geoffrey Dobbie had never been out of touch; he would travel from Devon when he could get his daughter to look after the sick wife who needed his whole attention. Afterwards, when she had died, he turned to me as the one consoler. Knowing he was in love, I could not hurt him. It would be out of the question for us to live together permanently, but I reasoned that he might be someone to have around, someone to care for me. I was wrong. When he did stay in the flat it was catastrophic. We had nothing in common. His ideas maddened me: there were two things he would not tolerate, the Young and the Blacks, and we argued until I thought I might get violent.

One summer evening an old friend who was visiting London took me out to dine. It had been gloriously reminiscent. As we were walking quietly back to Drayton Gardens, I asked him to come up. No key – of course – and I had to ask Geoffrey, on the 'blower', to let me in.

'Are you alone?' said the voice down the tube.

'No,' I answered. 'Someone is with me.'

'Then you can't come up unless you are alone.'

'Don't be crazy, Geoffrey,' I cried. 'It's *my* flat!' Meanwhile, my companion who had gathered what was wrong, said resignedly as he walked away down the path, 'Never mind, Eileen! I was always in the back row of the chorus.' At that point Geoffrey let me in and I raged at him. What right had he to behave like this? I must say he had not meant it; but jealousy defeated him. If he couldn't have me, then no one else must. Later he found a boarding-house where he could have bed and breakfast. Even so, he continued to be around the flat all day until he became really ill and a specialist I knew arranged for him to enter hospital.

VII

While I was at Drayton Gardens – it would have been during the spring of 1966 – I heard from Helene Weigel, widow of the dramatist Bertolt Brecht. She asked me to be her guest at an irresistible première, Sean's *Purple Dust* played by Brecht's Berliner Ensemble, probably then the best company in Europe. I got my permit, and at the East Berlin airfield two officials, one from the theatre, one representing the arts, cut away any red tape. I was driven to the sort of hotel common to most capital cities, and later to the theatre where Helene Weigel had left a corsage of flowers (a gift repeated with variations every evening). It was an almost extravagantly mounted performance. The technicians had got over the difficult climax when the ceiling gradually breaks and water floods down upon the stage: 'Th' little heap of purple dust they left behind them will vanish away in the flow of the river.' Finally, the river itself: 'Poges disappears down the passage as the green waters tumble into the room through the entrance from the hall.' The Ensemble acted superbly, and Sean's symbolism came through clearly in what was apparently a good translation that had replaced one much poorer. I noticed in this theatre that when the artists had been applauded, the stage-hands, wearing uniform jackets, also took their call; after the intricacies of *Purple Dust* they deserved it.

I had few chances to go beyond the theatre group. Actors, like all artists in East Germany, were treated admirably. Members of the Ensemble, once they had passed the entrance test, had a secure job; because there was no financial pressure, every production could be rehearsed for a long time. Two of Sean's plays, *Hall of Healing* and *The Moon Shines on Kylenamoe*, were also on at the Deutsche Theater; and, talking to the cast, I heard again how bad the earliest printed translations had been. One example. *Hall of Healing* is set in the waiting-room of a parish dispensary in Dublin; it is implied that the doctor drinks, and one of the patients says in effect, 'The doctor's late this morning; he's had a drop.' In the German text this was rendered literally as, 'The doctor's late; he's been hanged.' It must have been odd to see him enter a few speeches afterwards.

I visited other towns: Leipzig, where Sean's works, with letters and photographs, were put out for me to see at the publishing house; and Cottbus, where *Red Roses For Me* was on at the theatre. We drove over from East Berlin, a long journey on a hot day through the flat, nearly treeless, country, past fields and fields of asparagus and strawberries. These and trout in plenty were on my hotel menu. Nearly every day I had them all: three of my favourite foods in so poor a country. (To be fair, some other things were extremely scarce.) Once or twice you could be cheerfully startled as on an evening when, worn out, with aching feet, I sank into a chair and said to the hotel waiter, 'Dry martini!' He bowed and returned obligingly with three (*drei*) on a tray. Downing one, I took the others to my room.

From Berlin I went to Paris where Tom Curtiss met me and we saw another *Purple Dust*, acted by the company of the Théâtre Nationale Populaire before an eager young audience. The production was much simpler than the German one, but as apt in its own style and with lovely performances of Stoke and Poges – one long and thin, one short and stout – whose world is to be 'a little cloud o' purple dust blown upon the wind.'

VIII

While Shivaun was on her college tour, she had written to me about her new friend, Larry Kenig, who had joined their company. Now, back in London, they wanted to stay with me in Drayton Gardens. Good though it was to see them, I was not yet myself. Because Sean had never been out of the house I missed him all the more; I had not stopped being sorry for myself and dwelling on my loss, and I could not have been very lively. Anyway. Shivaun and Larry would not have settled in so small a flat. Finding their own, they married and began to work on the stage.

Hating idleness, I saw that I must work myself. One possibility was a book about Sean. I had read several, some by people who might have spent half an hour or less with him. Critical books as well, some good, others not. I wanted to say what he was like as a person to live with, so I proposed this to Macmillan and in time received a contract. Further, since Sean died, inquiries had streamed in from students in America or on the Continent. Always prepared to answer questions, he must have written hundreds of letters to people, old or young, who loved his work enough to be inquisitive about it: an audience that had not seen his later plays. Though far less informed, I felt I must continue as he had done, so I engaged a typist, the correspondence went on growing, and today in my Irish home the letters still arrive.

CHAPTER SIXTEEN

Travelling

SEAN has a famous line in *Red Roses*: 'Isn't it a wondher, now, you wouldn't sing an Irish song, free o' blemish, instead o' one thickly speckled with th' lure of foreign enthertainment?' Getting my 'foreign enthertainment' by listening to Sean's plays in many languages, I continued to be a good European; the next stop was Czechoslovakia where O'Casey seemed to be conquering Prague. They had asked me there to look at Jiri Krijcik's exhilarating production of *Bedtime Story*, with a quite uncommon performance of the leading man by an actor named Vladimir Pucholt. Sean enjoyed writing *Bedtime Story*, and I enjoyed seeing it and meeting its Czech audiences, a friendly people with an elegance nothing could destroy. A first visit was brief (during it I saw the television films of *A Pound on Demand* and *The End of the Beginning*), but when Krijcik filmed *Bedtime Story* I went there again, to a large, conventional hotel on the outskirts of Prague. I was often at the studios or a central film club, and when not in the theatre I could drive out in the country to one of the great castles or walk at evening through that shining romantic city and beside its river.

Hearing one day that I was ill with a bad neck, stiffness and arthritis, Krijcik advised me to take the cure at Marienbad and to stay at an old-fashioned hotel in the hills, surrounded by pine forests. At the spa clinic, where the head doctor knew Sean's work, the plays and autobiographies, they treated me nobly. Edward the Seventh had taken the Marienbad waters more than sixty years earlier; in his time the hotel across the way must have been a grand affair. It is used now as a workers' hostel, a holiday home for those in need of treatment. The clinic is a magnificent place, large, many-floored, and full of steam baths, hot and cold blanket baths, special spa-water baths – my scene undoubtedly. Through a strenuous week I rose early, took three solemn draughts at ten-minute intervals from a fountain in the gardens – there are several, each for a different ailment – and submitted to a brigade of large, silent, white-gowned ladies in the clinic itself. We talked in sign language which appeared to be enough. Keeping, I hope, a mild friendly grin, I was introduced on various days to steam and blanket baths and to baths in the tingle of freshly running spa water. I remember having a hose played on me, front and back, being vigorously massaged, standing under a freezing shower, and performing all rites the large, silent ladies prescribed. One morning, as we were standing together, relaxed and cheerful, in a big room, I talked to a pair of slim, lovely girl patients who were German ballet dancers. (There were also some quite enormous women.) In the evenings at my hotel everyone danced. It was the week for a conference of dentists, unexpectedly light-hearted. Marienbad had been an experience; when I reached Prague again I felt that I had lost five or six pounds.

I travelled home through Paris to see Sean's publishers, and also Tom Curtiss, whose flat over the Tour d'Argent contained more books, in piles and mounds, than I had seen in any private house. He entertained me warmly; and I dined, too, with Samuel Beckett at a little restaurant he frequented: a shy man, he is at ease once he likes you and begins to talk. In some ways he reminds me of Sean, though without Sean's bursting humour. It was a mild night; we dined in the open and afterwards walked for a long time round Paris, talking about most things and pausing here and there at cafés to drink wine and to watch the people. I wanted to buy some good thin jerseys for Breon and my son-in-law; Sam promised to call next morning to go shopping, and though we had walked half over Paris and returned to the hotel very late, the receptionist woke me at nine by saying in an awed voice on the telephone, 'Madame O'Casey, Monsieur Samuel Beckett is below waiting for you.'

II

Sam had already had a play done at the English National Theatre. I was happy now when Sir Laurence Olivier chose *Juno* and directed it himself, lifting the set from *The Plough and the Stars*: 'The front and back drawing-rooms in a fine old Georgian house, struggling for life against the assaults of time and the more savage assaults of the tenants.' The National company acted this as I think Sean would have wished: Joyce Redman as Juno, Colin Blakely and Frank Finlay as the Paycock and Joxer, and Ronald Pickup bringing out Johnny's hysterical anguish as I had not known before. It moved me to remember how I had first read and seen the play: I hoped that its National reception, excited and exciting, might stir curiosity about the later work Sean had prized so much. Before its Old Vic opening *Juno* was briefly on tour. One evening, while walking in Birmingham with Olivier, and near the Repertory Theatre Sir Barry Jackson had founded, he recalled the seasons there in his youth. He had been in love with a girl who took absolutely no notice of him, preferring some other men in the company. To me it sounded incredible. Had she become a famous actress? 'No,' he said mildly, 'she married and left the stage. I don't honestly remember her name, but it was shattering at the time.'

At *Juno* I could not help thinking of all that had risen from that afternoon in a New York hotel, and the friends I had made through the years. One was Harold Macmillan, Sean's publisher. It was a joy to spend a week-end with him at Chelwood Gate in Sussex and to hear him talk freely of Sean and the Irish writers his house had published. He never spoke of his political life, only of plays he had seen and performances he had admired, the best in traditional drama. I noticed that sometimes he had Sean's habit of getting up to act his stories.

III

Presently I again met Krijcik, my Czech friend (a handsome man of between forty-five and fifty), when he came to London from Prague, hoping to sell the film of *Bedtime Story*. With his tiny allowance he had to put up in an inferior rooming-house near Victoria, so I said that he could have his meals in my flat and use it as his home by day when he was not at an appointment: he had brought with him a few things like sausage meat and cheese that his wife had packed to help him out. In London he knew a former Czech actress who accompanied him to interpret his talks with the League of Dramatists or the film agents. I am afraid *Bedtime Story*, which I saw at a trade-show, did lack something: its leading man in the stage production had moved from acting to medicine, and in spite of a lively cast, with a new principal, the film was inferior to the play; its humour seemed to me to be overdone and it was never booked for London.

Two of my friends asked Krijcik to dinner. We saw him afterwards to his rooming-house. Next day, in great nervous agitation, he said he dared not remain in his lodgings a night longer. The gas fire had gone wrong. He might have been asphyxiated. He was obliged to sleep with his window open. And so on at length – he was an excitable man. That evening we were invited to the opening of a club in Chelsea; it was after midnight when Krijcik realised he had nowhere to sleep and I invited him to come along and use the sofa in my sitting-room. He did, slept soundly, and at breakfast appeared to have been overwhelmed by the comfort of it all. Turning at the door, he hugged me, kissed my hand, and cried, 'Eileen, I had a really wonderful night. Such a night! . . . Oh, I thank you!' More hand-kissing and hugging. Julian Glover, from the flat above, was on the stairs. He looked at me and gave a wicked wink while Krijcik ran on volubly, 'It was wonderful. A lovely night, Eileen. I am so happy and refreshed.'

IV

My rent was so high in Drayton Gardens that it would plainly
make more sense if I could buy a flat or house on mortgage.
Except in Woronzow Road we had never owned a property;
but now I was pouring rent away and owning nothing. Geoffrey
Dobbie was in London; I still played with a notion that perhaps
he might look after the garden and be some sort of company
for me. In a stupid way I felt responsible for him, particularly
as he was resolved to stick. So I began to consider such towns as
Brighton, Guildford and Chichester where there was usually
some theatre, at least a good rep. – in the deeper country I
would have been lost. We used to set out in the morning after
glancing through advertisements in *Country Life* and the Sunday papers: Brighton I liked, near the Downs especially, but
though one house there tempted me, Geoffrey hated it, the
Downs and Brighton on sight. Indeed he groused so much that
I gave up, and successively he put the damper on Chichester
and Guildford. Fate again: it would have been crazy to live
with him anywhere, for we were always quarrelling.

At length I struck. It must be myself alone: London and a
flat upstairs and no garden for Geoffrey (I would have been
frightened, anyway, to sleep on a ground floor). Hampstead
appealed to me; I hit upon an upper maisonette in Cannon
Place, high in the village and with the Heath only round the
corner. Even if it was in a house, not a block, which affected
the mortgage, this would soon be resolved, and I could move
in. Not immediately, because I did need structural changes: a
wall knocked down to make a large kitchen-dining-room; a
wooden floor laid in one of the rooms; the bathroom (of course)
re-done. People asked why I had chosen a flat high up, with
many stairs and without a lift. 'Won't it be terrible, Eileen,
when you are older?' I said that while my heart kept going, the
exercise should do me good.

Since Shivaun was having a first baby any day, and I was

anxious to be close to her, I went into a hotel room not far from Swiss Cottage and its memories of Goldhurst Terrace. The work at Cannon Place trailed on – these things are always longer than you expect – and the move was typically grim. One of the men, an aggressive fellow, kept nipping whisky from the bottles on the sideboard. Everything seemed furiously disorganised; press-cuttings books I wanted were whirled off before I could speak, and they even packed the sandwiches we had made for lunch – these arrived at Cannon Place two months later, mouldy in the tin. But one morning the business was finished. My other furniture arrived from Harrods, and I was in: an amazing panoramic view from the top attic room when London lights were up in the evening and the Post Office tower gleamed in the middle distance. That, I said to myself, was that; I could stay in Hampstead until I died.

v

I did not guess what lay in front of me. Sean's work had been more and more popular in Europe and America during the last four years of his life, and death duties on the estate were enormous. When the money for the *Young Cassidy* film came in, we used the bulk of it to pay our debts and to renew the Torquay flat. To wipe off the duties with what remained was impossible, hence the demand for tax owing. Argument stretched out. I passed from one office to the next, walked corridors by the mile, saw tall men and short men, fat men and thin men, all ready to guarantee that they would do the best for me and that everything would be arranged. Soon afterwards, asking what the settlement was, I would be told that they were seeing to it, or possibly that they had never even heard of the affair; the documents had grounded in somebody's files.

Fat men and thin men apart, there was enough to do at Hampstead. While grappling with the emotional side of my life, I had neglected the book; now I got on with it more or less in longhand, though it was surprising how many people came in to type. After beginning on a tape-recorder I had given this up: it was the wrong kind of solo programme. To stand in the attic solemnly saying my piece made me feel eccentric, and I understood why Sean had been self-conscious at Torquay.

Glad to be near Shivaun and her first child Ruben, who was born at Charing Cross Hospital in May 1968, I used to go across on most days to see them. When Ruben was about four months old he developed scarlet fever. A little later, after dining out, I felt ill in a taxi on my journey home. I could hardly stir next morning with the pain in my side, and I seemed to have spots as well. Consulting my medical advisers in the health section of *Pears Cyclopaedia*, I matched my symptoms against theirs and decided that I had pleurisy and measles. Reading on, I found that a woman of mature age, after being with a child who had scarlet fever, could contract pleurisy and measles. Whereupon I telephoned the doctor and said, 'I am quite ill. I have pleurisy and measles.' Oh, really? he replied, but how could I know? I told him I had consulted *Pears Cyclopaedia*. Silence for a moment; he would come to see me. He did, and said reluctantly that I had pleurisy and measles.

Anna, a German woman, large and bossy, was helping in the flat just then, and Geoffrey called in every day. He had said, during our many arguments, 'You don't know what it's like to depend on anybody; if you were ill and I had to look after you, you might appreciate me more.' And here I was, ill in my charming attic room above Hampstead. It was agony to move; you had to laugh, or you would cry with the pain. No help whatever from Anna: she left the morning tea at the foot of the attic stairs and shouted up, 'Here's your tea, dear; I'm not coming up to catch anything.' And I had to crawl down the stairs to get it. Geoffrey, arriving about eleven o'clock, did as much as he could, though he spoiled it a little by saying, 'You see what it's like to have to depend on someone . . . but I am really far worse than you are.' Probably true, but not on the whole the moment to brag about it.

The measles left me without any sense of smell or taste, and with a singing voice out of tune. A specialist assured me that smell and taste would return, as they did, and maybe my singing, which did not. Certainly, about three years later, when I was trying over 'One Enchanted Evening' with an American friend, only heaven could tell what I sounded like. My partner did not enlarge on it.

VI

Geoffrey returned temporarily to Devon to see if he could settle near his children. Other men were entering my life. One of them was a Labour Member of Parliament I had met at a St Patrick's Day luncheon. His sense of humour fitted mine; I liked to lunch with him at the House of Commons and to have tea on the Terrace; but when we spent the whole day together I realised that this could not be permanent. As our friendship matured he proposed marriage, and it was lucky for both our sakes that the mood passed, though our friendship remained. A wine-merchant who took me out from both Drayton Gardens and Cannon Place was a generous person but humourless. He had visited us in Torquay and read everything Sean had written; and he would go anywhere to see an O'Casey performance, professional or amateur; he went, I remember, to Hornchurch where the repertory company put on the rarely-acted *The Drums of Father Ned*. What puzzled me was how he could appreciate the theatre so much when he had so little humour of his own.

In the end Geoffrey Dobbie chose to live in Norfolk. He became, I could see, genuinely ill; his doctors, refusing to diagnose anything, wrote him off as a grumpy and awkward hypochondriac. Invariably he had complained of his stomach. When I visited Norwich to help him move from a small hotel into a new flat and to arrange his books and china, his distress worried me so keenly that I called again on the doctor who had merely talked of premature old age. His niece Ada, who lived on a farm at Thurning, was as troubled as I was. Before getting back to London on the Monday, I had asked the doctor to examine Geoffrey; on the Wednesday Ada telephoned to say he had been taken to hospital, and when I returned to Norwich he was in a geriatric ward. Never, never, I hope, will I have to enter such a ward again: rows of old people, all of them doomed and knowing it, and rarely with any visitor to cheer them up.

Geoffrey was so ill that he could take no food. I begged the nursing Sister to let him see a specialist. 'Are you a close relative?' she asked; I explained the position, and on telephoning a few nights later, I found that Sister had responded and called in a specialist. Geoffrey, suffering from lung cancer, was in great pain and had had his first morphia injection that day. It was not long before Breon, who was staying with me in Cannon Place, took a telephone message: Geoffrey had died.

What can one say? I was happy, if that is the word, that the truth had been discovered and that his family would understand, as I did, that he was no tiresome old misanthrope but a man who had endured bravely. In a way I had one problem less, yet another person was out of my life. I had to miss him.

VII

Sean's manuscripts had been put on show in the New York Library. I was invited across to a sumptuous opening ceremony, and Robert and Marjorie Graff entertained me in their house at Far Hills, New Jersey – to my surprise, a foxhunting region: I had assumed the sport was wholly English and Irish. Next, with my friend Kathy Coker in Los Angeles, I was reminded again how American people love to entertain you in their own homes. In England later I began to be embarrassed whenever an American voice said on the telephone, 'Eileen, we are in London. Can we come along to see you?' Instead of saying yes at once, and letting them take me as I was, I would go into a panic, wonder what they could have to eat, how I could tidy the place up; usually it ended with mixed excuses and a meeting at a restaurant. It was a relief when I could grow out of this and ask them to come up to Cannon Place, which after all was what they wanted; you cannot get the picture unless you have seen the person at home.

From Los Angeles I moved to San Francisco where Lester Cole took me out to the ancient redwood forests, the world's tallest trees, among an intense, eerie silence so solid that you could almost catch hold of it. Thence with Kathy Coker to Mexico, which I had long wanted to visit; its heat and dust, its blazing flowers and masses of roses, and the poverty that seemed deceptively less when you saw those people lying out in the sunshine, dark-eyed, white-haired women, enchanting children. From our stay with the Cedric Belfrages in Cuernavaca I remember now a bedroom balcony where the tiles practically scorched your feet if you were shoeless. In the distance was the cone of an active volcano which burned with a light like a small candle as you looked over to it in the cool of the evening.

CHAPTER SEVENTEEN

Back to Dublin

At home in Cannon Place, where I looked across a London evening to the lights of the Post Office Tower, it disheartened me to find a set of income-tax demands: sheer chaos, I thought, as I toured the usual departments, explaining to the usual men why, as usual, I was not paying everything I owed. Royalties that had accumulated in East Germany could now be transferred to England, and as Sean's plays had been in production over there for so many years, the money arrived in a lump sum. It was always pleasant to receive money and to know that Sean's work was being performed. It was unpleasant because, as unearned income, most of it would go in tax. Buff envelopes, in assorted sizes, were pushed daily through my letter-box at 9 Cannon Place and the demands grew frightening.

My book *Sean* had been finished at the end of 1970. Eager to work, I returned to the idea of teaching backward children to read. But on the appearance of *Sean* the publisher suggested a companion, more especially on my own life, and this began to absorb me. True, it was not so absorbing that I could overlook the problem of my tax debts. Wondering briefly about life in Switzerland, I did have a short holiday with Sean's Swiss publisher in Zurich: a beautiful country, but among all that wealth my tax problems would have looked absurd. It was ironic that during Sean's life we had had to struggle to pay tax and live on his small income. Now, after his death, his works were earning sums we would have been eager to get when the children were young. And I was still struggling to keep up with the tax.

I was advised finally to live in Ireland where at least all I got from writing would be my own. With Shivaun and Ruben I crossed to investigate; an old friend, J. J. O'Leary, put us up in Dublin, and during the entire week it poured. Remembering then how, during our honeymoon, we had dined at Dalkey with Lennox Robinson of the Abbey Theatre and his wife Dolly, I told J.J. that I would like to see the house again, Sorrento Cottage, above its own tiny beach. He demurred, 'Don't you think it's a little large, Eileen?' But I would not be put off until I had telephoned the owner, told him that I wanted to revive romantic memories, and discovered, when he invited me one morning, how big the 'cottage' really was: within a few years it was sold for an immense sum. Though nothing emerged from that week's exploration in the rain, I took a furnished flat in the winter of 1971, continued to search, and eventually and gratefully came upon the place I needed: a small, gently elegant house from which I could explore again the city we had known very early in our married life.

Sad though it was to leave London and all it meant, some force was impelling me to go. Sean had said in that last talk on the day he died, 'You should live in America, Eileen, where you have so many friends . . . or maybe in Paris.' What he meant was that I should begin afresh. I have yet to see why fate has sent me to Dublin; but I have my house, I have made good friends, and I find myself enjoying the slower pace, an entirely new existence which stops me from dwelling on the past. Loneliness (and what I call 'aloneness') are not for me; even now, if nobody is in at night, the stillness can trouble me. No matter: my small house is there, I like it, and whenever I return to it I can be sure that it is welcoming me home.

Index

O'Casey, Sean : – (cont.)
Totnes, 143–73; describes Totnes in *West Country Magazine*, 148–9; the evacuees, 151; reads from *Finnegans Wake* at Dartington, 161; pleads for repertory company, 162; agitation at being left, 162–3; goes up to *Red Roses*, 164; disappointed by *Oak Leaves* production, 165–7; *Life* pictorial feature, 172–3; Torquay, 174–91; feeding the birds, 175; NBC film, 176–7; Niall's death, 179–81; *Cock-a-doodle Dandy* in London, 185–6; at eighty, 187; letter to Trinity College, Dublin, 189–90; death, 191–2; cremation, 193–4
O'Casey, Shivaun (Mrs Laurence Kenig): 16, 152, 153, 156, 158–9, 160, 163–5, 169–72, 173, 177, 181, 186, 188, 191–6, 202–3, 208–9, 210, 215
O'Farrell, Margaret, 89
O'Leary, J. J., 215
Olivier, Sir Laurence (Lord Olivier), 206
O'Malley, Mary, 187
O'Neill, Carlotta, 133
O'Neill, Eugene, 131–2; 133
O'Neill, Maire, 81, 83–4, 89
O'Regan, Kathleen, 81, 83–5

Paris, 160–72, 202, 205–6
Parsons, Lady, 47
Patience (Gilbert and Sullivan), 56
Philadelphia, 75–6
Phillpotts, Eden, 87
Pickup, Ronald, 206
Pictures in the Hallway (O'Casey autobiography), 157; stage reading, 175
Pirates of Penzance, The (Gilbert and Sullivan), 56
Plough and the Stars, The (O'Casey), 67, 83–6, 88, 90, 94, 100, 112, 163
Plymouth, 153–5, 157, 186
Pound on Demand, A (O'Casey), 130–1, 202

Pounds, Courtice, 63, 118
Pounds, Mary, 63, 118–19
Prague, 204–5, 207
Priestley, J. B., 161
Private Lives (Coward), 161
Pucholt, Vladimir, 204
Purple Dust (O'Casey), 14, 143; Wanamaker's production, 168–9; East Berlin, 201; Paris, 202

Redman, Joyce, 206
Red Roses For Me (O'Casey), 14, 17, 157–8, 202, 204; London production, 162–4
Reynolds, Kathleen (Eileen's mother; *née* Kathleen Carey): marriage and Eileen's birth in Dublin, 20; London lodgings, 20; as nurse-companion, 22; appearance, 25; husband's death, 28; Eileen's school uniform, 34–5; relationship with Eileen, 35–6; at Wivelsfield Green, 44; retires from work, 45; drinks, 46, 48; discovers Eileen at Swiss Cottage, 49; Brighton, 60, 71; St Andrew's Mansions, 71; again with Eileen, and quarrel, 89–90; calls on Sean, 93; at Eileen's wedding, 97; at Chalfont, 129; at Torquay, 151; lodging at Paignton, 167; ill at Torquay, 178–9; death and funeral, 184–5
Rhondda, Viscountess, 132
Rice, Elmer, 133
Riders to the Sea (Synge), 88–9
Robinson, Lennox, 94, 117, 215
Rose and Crown (O'Casey autobiography), 69, 109, 117
Rose Marie (music, Rudolf Friml, Herbert Stothart), 67–71, 75, 87, 90, 95, 119; 'Totem Tom Tom', 68
Ruth (parlourmaid), at Battersea, 140–2; at Totnes, 145–6

St Bartholomew's Hospital, London, 180–1
Saint Joan (Shaw), 182
St Ives, Cornwall, 178, 181, 191, 198